D1286611

DELINQUENTS
IN THE MAKING

OTHER BOOKS BY THE AUTHORS

by Sheldon and Eleanor Glueck

Five Hundred Criminal Careers
One Thousand Juvenile Delinquents
Five Hundred Delinquent Women
Later Criminal Careers
Juvenile Delinquents Grown Up
Criminal Careers in Retrospect
After-conduct of Discharged Offenders
Preventing Crime (Editors)
Unraveling Juvenile Delinquency

by Eleanor Touroff Glueck

The Community Use of Schools
Extended Use of School Buildings
Evaluative Research in Social Work

by Sheldon Glueck

Mental Disorder and the Criminal Law
Crime and Justice
War Criminals: Their Prosecution and Punishment (transl. into Spanish)
The Nuremburg Trial and Aggressive War (transl. into Japanese)
Probation and Criminal Justice (Editor)
Cases on Criminal Law (Editor; with Livingston Hall)
Criminal Law and Enforcement (Editor; with Livingston Hall)
Crime and Correction: Selected Papers

DELINQUENTS
In The Making

Paths To Prevention

by
SHELDON & ELEANOR GLUECK

WITHDRAWN

HARPER & BROTHERS-PUBLISHERS-NEW YORK

To
ROSCOE POUND
who taught us that
the "law in books"
can often be greatly illuminated
by investigation into
the law in action

DELINQUENTS IN THE MAKING

Copyright, 1952, by Harper & Brothers
Printed in the United States of America

All rights in this book are reserved. No part of the book may be used or re-produced in any manner whatsoever without written permission except in the case of brief quotations embodied in critical articles and reviews. For information address Harper & Brothers, 49 East 33rd Street, New York 16, N. Y.

E-B

Library of Congress catalog card number: 51-11917

Contents

Preface

This little volume is the outgrowth of a widespread request for a simpler version of the findings of the research into persistent delinquency published in *Unraveling Juvenile Delinquency* (New York: The Commonwealth Fund, 1950). Most of the materials are presented in less technical language, but here and there we have included whole passages from the original volume. Certain materials in the present book do not appear in the more extensive work; namely, Chapter III, entitled "Meet Frankie and Jimmy," a further development of causal theory, and additional suggestions for the prevention and control of juvenile delinquency. And some materials from the larger work have been omitted entirely as they are of interest only to specialists.

The research that has served as the basis for *Unraveling Juvenile Delinquency* was carried out by us under the auspices of the Harvard Law School, and with a large staff of associates and assistants. It was begun in 1940, the field work completed in 1948, and the findings published in 1950. This is part of a continuing research program into various aspects of the causes, treatment, and prevention of crime.

We are deeply grateful to The Commonwealth Fund, which published the larger work, for permitting us to make use of the findings in this more popular presentation.

A statistical inquiry can, perforce, deal only with a sample of the whole. This unavoidable fact immediately lays any research open to facile criticism. The test of the validity of a sample is the extent to which it is "typical" of the facts embraced in the problem defined for inquiry. Because this is a study of persistent delinquents from underprivileged areas, it cannot directly shed light on delinquents in the more favorably circumstanced classes of society. However, granting that some children of well-to-do parents are delinquent but do not as frequently get into the courts, delinquency remains essentially a mode of behavior most frequently found among the economically submerged classes.

We wish to repeat from the Preface to *Unraveling Juvenile Delinquency*: "This book represents the first analysis of the data; further reflection, particularly examination of more intimate intercorrelations of the constituents of the various levels of exploration, will very probably bring about deeper insights and some modification of present conclusions."

Just as there is no royal road to learning, so is there no king's highway to the heart of the problem of crime causation. The research on which this book is based makes no pretense to finality. It is a first approximation to a scientific assessment of the causal influences making for persistent delinquency in the underprivileged neighborhoods of our large cities.

Our appreciation is due to our secretary, Esther Ghostlaw, for her skill and patience in frequent retypings of this manuscript.

SHELDON AND ELEANOR GLUECK

Harvard Law School
Cambridge, Mass.
September, 1951

DELINQUENTS
IN THE MAKING

With ready-made opinions one cannot judge of crime. Its philosophy is a little more complicated than people think. It is acknowledged that neither convict prisons, nor the hulks, nor any system of hard labour ever cured a criminal.

—Dostoevsky, *The House of the Dead,* Part I, Chapter 2.

CHAPTER I

Let's Stop Guessing About Juvenile Delinquency

The readiness of lay and professional persons to explain the origins of deviant character and criminal conduct without taking a *comprehensive* view has been a chief obstacle to the discovery of the factors really involved in antisocial behavior. Malformation of character—that human disorder most difficult to understand and remedy—has all too often been accounted for by simplistic explanations or professional dogmas or propagandistic enthusiasms. The result has been that society's institutions designed to deal with crime—its laws, courts, prisons, and preventive programs—have not been built on a sufficiently reliable factual foundation.

No wonder, therefore, that the great majority of youths who have had juvenile court and reformatory treatment carry their antisocial attitudes and behavior right along into adult life. No wonder, either, that on the whole "crime preventives" have not been too successful in sweeping back the tide of delinquency and crime.

We know much more today, however, about the impulsions and surrounding conditions of juvenile delinquency than we did fifty years ago. Beginning with Healy's path-blazing *The Individual Delinquent,* and including the contributions of Burt, Lindner, Shaw, the pioneers in child guidance, such as Bronner, Bernard Glueck, and Kenworthy, and other workers in clinics and institutions, much light has been shed on the intricate processes of maladapted behavior. (It is unfortunate that too little of this has as yet actually penetrated into channels for administering justice.)

Some insight into the causation of delinquency and crime can be obtained from almost any approach that bears a reasonable relationship to the nature of the problem. Even meteorology can contribute; investigations have been made which show seasonal and climatic variations in crime and delinquency. There are numerous studies, especially on the European continent, of fluctuations in various indexes of economic conditions (prices of basic commodities, business activity, and the like) as related to the ups and downs of crime or delinquency. Approaching somewhat closer to the core of the problem, many studies have been made of the relationship of neighborhood conditions to crime. Coming still closer, there have been studies of specific factors of environment and culture, such as culture conflict, bad companions, dearth of adequate recreational facilities, and the like. On the other hand, there have been investigations emphasizing the genetic and constitutional origins of persistent criminalism, from the works of Lombroso and his precursors, involving variations on the theme of the born criminal, atavism, degeneration, and epilepsy, to the traditional psychiatric studies that emphasize psychoses and psychopathic personality. Finally, in recent years there have been a few psychoanalytic investigations and numerous studies (usually based on inadequate samples) of various individual psychologic, emotional, or characteral elements or patterns.

By and large, examination of existing researches in juvenile delinquency discloses a tendency to overemphasize a particular approach or explanation. Proponents of various theories of causation still too often insist that the truth is to be found only in their own special fields of study and that, *ex hypothesi,* researches made by those working in other disciplines can contribute little to the understanding and management of the crime problem.

Yet it stands to reason that, since so little is as yet known about the intricacies of normal human behavior, it is the better part of wisdom not to be overawed by any branch of science or methodology to the neglect of other promising leads in the study of aberrant behavior. When, therefore, research into the causes of delinquency emphasizes the sociologic, or ecologic, or cultural, or psychiatric, or psychoanalytic, or anthropologic approach, relegating the others to a remote position, if not totally ignoring them, we must immediately be on guard. The problems of human motivation and behavior involve the study of man as well as society, of nature as well as nurture, of segments or "mechanisms" of the human mind as well as the total personality, of patterns of intimate social activity as well as larger areas of social process or masses of culture. They must, therefore, be studied through *the participation of several disciplines.* Without recognition of this fact, bias must weaken the validity of both method and interpretation.

For example, a weakness or an incompleteness of much sociologic reasoning on the causal processes in crime is the assumption that the mass social stimulus to behavior, as reflected in the particular culture of a region, is alone, or primarily, the significant causal force. This presupposition ignores two undeniable facts: first, that in every society— whether largely rural or largely urban, whether agricultural or industrial, whether composed essentially of one ethnic group or of many, or of a consistent culture or several clashing ones, whether existing at one historic period or another— there have been individuals who would not or could not conform to the taboos and laws prohibiting particular forms of behavior; secondly, and relatedly, that differences exist in the responses of various individuals or classes of persons to many of the elements in the culture-complex of a region.

The true significance of the factors dealt with by the area sociologist can be determined only through close study of the points of impact of social forces upon *individuals* of varying *biologic make-up and childhood conditioning*. The varieties of physical, mental, and social make-up of different persons must determine, in large measure, the way in which they will be influenced by social disorganization, culture conflict, and the growing pains of the city. To overemphasize the neighborhood matrix as a coherent whole and underemphasize or virtually ignore the biologic make-up and childhood developmental history of the different human beings who themselves contribute to the modification of that matrix is to overlook many of the factors that account for variations in the effect of the culture on human beings and thereby to distort reality with reference not only to the causal problem but even to the nature of the culture in question.

The same enthusiastic emphasis on a single approach to crime causation—this time involving the economic factor of poverty—is to be found in many European studies of crime; and it has proved equally sterile and distorted. Since poverty operates differently on various types of persons, it should be obvious that something more than poverty (or unemployment, or the fluctuations in the price of some standard commodity, or the vicissitudes of the business cycle) must be examined before the role of poverty in the genesis of delinquency and crime can be understood.

Unilateral study of the causes of delinquency and criminalism is not confined to some sociologists and economists. Such an approach has also existed on the part of proponents of various biologic theories. Lombroso's belated recognition of the operation of sociolgic factors was submerged in his persistent enthusiasm for the theory that crime is often the natural activity of persons destined from birth, by virtue of atavism (hereditary reversion or throwback to some remote ancestry), to become criminal. More recently, some enthusiastic endocrinologists have also made claims for the exclusiveness or primacy of glandular dysfunction as the causal agency in delinquency, without recognizing that any one-sided approach is a distortion of reality. Psychoanalytic explanations of delinquency are also inclined to an overemphasis on a single point of view. But the general acceptance of the role of early environmental conditioning upon the development of personality and character tends to make psychoanalysts recognize the importance of both biologic and cultural forces and of the interchanging influences of endowment and nurture in the genesis of maladapted behavior.

Other illustrations could be given of the tendency toward one-sided study of the causes of delinquency which springs from specialization in some particular science or method. But enough has been said to indicate that this is a pitfall which we have made every effort to avoid in the planning and execution of a research designed to throw light on the complexities of the causal process in delinquency.

At the present stage of knowledge a many-sided approach to the study of human motivation and behavior is obviously necessary. It is clear that such an inquiry should be designed to reveal meaningful integrations of diverse data from several levels of inquiry.

There has long been a need for a *systematic* approach that would not ignore any promising leads to crime causation, covering as many fields and utilizing as many of the most reliable and relevant techniques of investigation and measurement as are necessary for a fair sampling of the various aspects of a complex biosocial problem.

While the most promising areas of research in human conduct and misconduct are to be found in the nexus of physical and mental functions and in the interplay of person and milieu, the complexities of motivation and varieties of behavior compel a division of the field into areas or levels. These must be interpreted serially before arriving at a meaningful integrated pattern. In this book we shall acquaint the reader with some basic factors involved in the development of children into what society labels "juvenile delinquents."

Before proceeding further, we should define the concept of delinquency as used in the research on which this book is based. Any child who commits even a single minor act in violation of the law is technically a delinquent. In Massachusetts, for example, a "delinquent child" is one "between seven and seventeen who violates any city ordinance or town bylaw or commits an offense not punishable by death." A "wayward child" is one "between seven and seventeen years of age who habitually associates with vicious or immoral persons, or who is growing up in circumstances exposing him to lead an immoral, vicious or criminal life."[5]

For the purposes of the research upon which this volume is based, however, delinquency refers to *repeated* acts of a kind which when committed by persons beyond the statutory juvenile court age are punishable as crimes (either felonies or misdemeanors)—except for a few instances of *persistent* stubbornness, truancy, running away, associating with immoral persons, and the like.

Children who once or twice during the period of growing up in an excitingly attractive milieu steal a toy in a ten-cent store, sneak into a subway or motion picture theatre, play

[5] Acts and Resolves of Massachusetts, 1948, Ch. 310, Sec. 3. At the time the research project on which this book is based was begun, children committing an offense punishable by life imprisonment were excluded from the jurisdiction of the juvenile court.

hooky, and the like and soon outgrow such peccadilloes are not true delinquents even though, technically, they have violated the law. Indeed, it is nowadays recognized that a certain amount of petty pilfering occurs among many children around the age of six or seven and is to be expected as part of the process of trying their wings.[6] Children appear to be no worse for very occasional and slight experimental deviations from socially acceptable norms of conduct. Since they soon voluntarily abandon such behavior, their misconduct or maladaptation cannot be deemed either habitual or symptomatic of deep-rooted causes.[7]

The legal definition of juvenile delinquency does not completely coincide with that used by the psychiatrist working in a clinic with children who present various emotional and behavior problems. But it is that interpretation of delinquency with which society, through its laws, concerns itself at a stage in a child's maladjustment where not only he himself is in danger but his acts are deemed to endanger the general security.

The analysis of the causes of juvenile delinquency is important not merely in itself and because of the immediate and more obvious trouble it gives society, but also because of the more general threat it represents. For the majority of adult criminals began their antisocial careers as child delinquents. Moreover, apart from the obvious harm dealt society by adult criminals, there is the more distant but real danger implicit in the fact that some of the more striking traits that mark delinquents are similar to the characteristic traits of Nazi,

6 A. Gesell and F. L. Ilg, *The Child from Five to Ten,* New York, Harper & Brothers, 1946, pp. 127, 156.

7 Compare Burt's definition: "A child is to be regarded as technically a delinquent when his antisocial tendencies appear so grave that he becomes, or ought to become, the subject of official action." C. Burt, *The Young Delinquent,* 4th Ed., London, University of London Press, 1944, p. 15. See, also, P. Tappan, *Juvenile Delinquency,* New York, McGraw-Hill Book Company, Inc., 1949, pp. 30, 32, 70.

Fascist, or Communist leaders. Without pursuing this line of inquiry, it is sufficient to remind the reader that if ever there was a field in which it is important to remember that "the child is father to the man" it is in the area of juvenile delinquency.

CHAPTER II

Need for Basic Facts

The riddle of crime is so puzzling that to arrive at adequate explanations calls for the collaboration of many sciences. Unless we keep an open mind and dig for facts in all areas that may reasonably be expected to throw some light upon it, we are likely to repeat the classic error of the blind men and the elephant of the fable; each of them believed the elephant to be formed like the particular piece of that animal which he happened to have touched.

It must, further, be emphasized that, unless we measure delinquents against a yardstick of nondelinquents, we are likely to be led astray in our conclusions. For example, a judge may have before him a succession of five or six juvenile offenders in a single day whose families are in dire poverty. He may therefore conclude that poverty is the sole or at any rate the chief cause of their antisocial behavior. But for each delinquent who comes from economically underprivileged homes a law-abiding youngster can be produced whose family also is handicapped by inadequate income.

It has long been claimed by psychoanalysts that people frequently commit crimes because driven by a subconscious feeling of guilt and a "need for punishment." Yet it remains to be demonstrated that such a mental mechanism in itself causes criminalism; nor has it been proved that it plays a role in a large proportion of criminal careers. Those who have seen re-

9

vealed the multiplicity and the complex interplay of forces
inside and outside the person that are involved in a career of
criminalism can only regard as a grossly unwarranted over-
simplification the view that the guilt feeling and subconscious
desire for punishment play a dominant role in typical delinquent and criminal behavior. The same may be said of other
one-sided and oversimplified "explanations" of criminalism.

Caution against arriving at conclusions on one-sided evidence may be given in respect to any trait or condition that
happens to come to mind because of the apparent frequency of
its occurrence among juvenile offenders. Delinquents and
other "problem children" are sometimes referred to as "deviates." But to know if a child deviates in any respect, one
must know what he deviates from; otherwise, a seemingly abnormal trait, which may be seized upon as a dramatic explanation of a tendency to delinquency, may in fact appear just
as often among nondelinquents.

Matching 500 Delinquents with 500 Nondelinquents

To avoid pitfalls, we designed an investigation in which we
compared 500 persistently delinquent boys ranging in age
from eleven to seventeen, with 500 truly nondelinquent boys,
matching them boy for boy by age, ethnic (racial) derivation,
general intelligence, and residence in underprivileged urban
neighborhoods.

In order to dissect a phenomenon like crime, one must
study a more or less fixed or systematic pattern of misbehavior.
It is for this reason that we deliberately selected *persistent*
delinquents. Some insist that all delinquents deserve study, a
point of view with which we have no quarrel. But in order to
probe root causes, we must study a more or less fixed course
of conduct rather than a transient and very common childhood phenomenon. As we pointed out in the previous
chapter, occasional childhood lapses from conventional be-

havior are quite common. When a child who once or twice steals a toy from a ten-cent store is brought into a juvenile court, this peccadillo may or may not be significant of a deeply rooted maladjustment to the restraints of the legal code. But the majority of children who occasionally experiment with misconduct abandon such behavior even without the aid of social workers, probation officers, or others. It is at least partial habituation in antisocial conduct that really sets off the delinquent boy from others; and it is therefore this type of lad who should be contrasted with the general run of boys.

Thorough investigation of the 500 nondelinquents revealed that a fourth of them had misbehaved to the extent, for example, of smoking in their early years, hopping trucks, once or twice "swiping" much-desired articles from the counters of a five-and-ten-cent store. One in ten had tried "crap-shooting," sneaked into movies, occasionally truanted from school, or were described by their mothers as being stubborn. A small proportion kept late hours, a few used vile language, a handful drank, or ran away from home, or bunked out, and so on. But such misconduct proved to be very occasional or accidental and was quickly abandoned. Indeed, it would almost seem that while some types of children are criminalized by early experiences with delinquency, others are immunized thereby.

On the other hand, the 500 delinquents had an official history of persistent and serious delinquency. Over half (59%) of them had been charged with burglary (including attempted burglary and intent to commit burglary); 58% with various forms of larceny (excluding larceny of automobiles); 20% with larceny of auto; 32% with crimes against the public order; 16% with "stubbornness"; 17% with running away; 13% with truancy; 5% with assault and battery; 4% with sex offenses; 2% each with robbery, arson, and drunkenness.

The average age of the delinquents at the time of their first court appearance proved to be 12.4 years; their average age at first conviction, 12.5 years. A little over a fourth of the boys first appeared in juvenile court when they were under eleven; another 46% at eleven, twelve, or thirteen years. Their average number of court appearances was 3.6, and their average number of convictions, 3.4.

In addition to their record of official delinquencies, as determined by court appearances, arrests, convictions, and commitments, a study in retrospect of the first clear signs of the delinquents' social maladaptation—stealing, truancy, destructive mischief, stubbornness, tantrums, disobedience, running away, stealing rides, junking, sex affairs, and the like—reveals that nearly half of them showed evidences of maladaptation before their eighth year and another two-fifths before their eleventh year, making a total of 88% whose antisocial conduct was already unmistakable before puberty. The average age at the onset of their antisocial behavior proved to be 8.3 years, in contrast with the average age of 12.4 years at their first court appearance.

From the foregoing analysis there can be little doubt of the seriousness and persistency of the misconduct of the 500 delinquents who are the subjects of our inquiry.

Why did we match the delinquents with the nondelinquents in respect to age, general intelligence, ethnic derivation, and residence in underprivileged urban neighborhoods?

The reason is that the factors that must be analyzed in order to dig to the roots of delinquency are so numerous that a way had to be found to avoid confusion. In order to study a large enough sample of variables certain other sets of factors must first be "held constant." In deciding which such factors to equalize among the two groups in pairing off delinquents and nondelinquents as a first step toward their later detailed comparison, we have been guided by several aims. First, since the ultimate comparison should cover subtle processes of personality and environment, the more general or cruder factors should be controlled in the matching; second, those traits which typically affect a whole range of factors ought to be held constant; third, those general characteristics which have already been explored sufficiently by other investigators and about which there is much agreement ought to be equalized in the two groups. Overriding all these aims, however, was the practical difficulty of matching two series of hundreds of human beings.

Scope of the Inquiry

By equating the 500 delinquent boys with the 500 non-delinquents in respect to age, general intelligence, ethnic derivation, and residence in underprivileged neighborhoods, we were free to compare them with regard to hundreds of other factors. Thereby we have avoided two pitfalls: (a) we have used a "control group" as a means of determining whether a seemingly abnormal trait or characteristic does in reality exist just as frequently among nondelinquents and therefore must, from the point of view of cause-and-effect, be deemed *neutral;* and (b) we have set the stage for a detailed comparison of delinquents and nondelinquents at so many levels of inquiry—family, school, and neighborhood life; physique, health; constituents of general intelligence; traits of temperament, personality, and character structure—that we have minimized the danger of one-sided explanations of the causes of juvenile crime.

In making this broad-gauged and deep-probing inquiry no pains or time have been spared to check on hundreds of facts from many angles. The full account of how this was accomplished will be found in *Unraveling Juvenile Delinquency.* The reader may wish to consult that volume for details beyond the scope of our present writing. Here we can only briefly describe the various aspects of the research.

(a) FAMILY AND PERSONAL BACKGROUND. First of all, we

sought as complete a picture as possible of the kinds of homes and families from which the two groups of boys stemmed. To this end it was necessary to reconstruct from many recorded sources the history of delinquency and criminalism; of alcoholism and mental deficiency; of emotional disturbances and serious physical ailments not only of the members of the boys' immediate families but also of grandparents and uncles and aunts. We also examined into the educational and the economic status of parents and grandparents. The aim of this probing into the past was to determine the conditions under which the parents of the two groups of boys had been reared, a state of affairs which in turn must have influenced the ideals, attitudes, and practices that *they* brought to the task of child rearing.

The cultural, psychologic, and emotional conditions in the homes of the boys were in turn subjected to intensive study. Still another aspect of this portion of our exploration dealt with the boys' habits and use of leisure. Attention here was especially directed to the age at which deviating behavior began and the nature of the earliest signs of antisocial conduct. Further, a detailed history of each boy's progress in school, as well as an assessment of the various forms of his school misbehavior, were secured.

So much for the contents of the inquiry into family and personal life. Intensive and extensive as this was, it yielded only a rough landscape of the soil in which the human plant— benign or malign—had grown. Before any conclusions could be drawn about why it turned "poisonous," a penetrating examination had to be made of the plant itself.

(b) BODILY TYPES. First, we examined the body structure and form of the boys. In selecting the most acceptable method of comparing delinquents and nondelinquents from the point of view of their physiques we were influenced by the work of Dr. William H. Sheldon (*Varieties of Human Phy-*

sique, New York, Harper & Brothers, 1942), based on the pioneering researches of Kretschmer. Each of the thousand boys was photographed in three positions (front, side, rear) according to a standardized method. The necessary anthropometric data were then derived from detailed measurement of these photographs, and classification was made in respect to fundamental bodily patterns (somatotypes). Somatotypes are classifiable according to the predominance of one of the three root-components that have entered into their development: *endomorphy,* in which soft roundness of the various regions of the body predominates; *mesomorphy,* in which muscle, bone, and connective tissue are conspicuous; and *ectomorphy,* characterized by the relative emphasis of linearity and fragility of bodily form. The extreme endomorph is the roundish, fat individual; the mesomorph is the closely knit, muscular, athletic type; the ectomorph is rather tall and thin.

The importance of comparing delinquents and nondelinquents in terms of bodily types arises from the fact that the dominance of one or another of the three components of bodily structure may well imply basic variations in energy output and temperament.

(c) HEALTH. Everyone would agree that a significant comparison of delinquents and nondelinquents should also include a *medical examination.* We wished to learn about the general state of health and gross evidence of disease of the delinquents and nondelinquents at the time they were taken on for study, since poor health is often alleged to be a significant causal factor in both behavior and disposition.

(d) INTELLIGENCE. It is commonly accepted that the hows and whys of human behavior are partly governed by the degree and quality of *intelligence* of individuals. Since one of the bases of the original matching of the 500 delinquents with the 500 nondelinquents was *general* intelligence in terms of I.Q., we took the opportunity to compare the delinquents with the nondelinquents in respect to the various *elements* entering into their general intelligence. Two boys of like I.Q. can have quite varying intellectual qualities in terms of individual mental traits.

(e) TEMPERAMENT AND CHARACTER STRUCTURE.   In recent years, those who have studied the human mind and behavior have concluded that the *emotional life* of the individual and, especially, the feeling-laden experiences of the first few years have a great deal to do with the structuring of character and the channeling of behavior. To get at the main features of character structure, various "projective" tests have been evolved. The Rorschach ("ink-blot") Test which we applied is one of the most frequently used and among the most penetrating and reliable of such revealers of the foundations of character.

In addition to this, an interview by a skilled psychiatrist was carried on with each boy. This revealed the more obvious personality traits of the boys, their many emotional stresses and conflicts and how they resolved them, and provided some insight into the reasons for the persistent misbehavior of the delinquents and the law-abidingness of the other lads.

In order to avoid circular reasoning and unconscious bias, and to permit of the proper assessment of the contribution of each avenue of approach to the mosaic of crime causation, the data of each portion of the research were gathered independently of every other. For example, at no time did the psychiatrist who interviewed the boys have access to the Rorschach or other findings; nor did those who compiled the family and personal histories know the findings emerging from other portions of the inquiry.

Procedures

Even this sketchy account of the different ways in which the two groups of boys were examined shows that anyone wishing to make more than a superficial study of the causes of human maladjustment must start with the assumption that there is no single road to an understanding of the problem.

Extending over a ten-year period from the formulation of the inquiry to its completion, the work has involved many associates and assistants, both in tapping innumerable sources of data and in following through countless details. The continued cooperation of many public and voluntary welfare agencies and officials had to be enlisted in order to gather all the needed facts about the thousand lads who parade through the following pages.

But apart from this, the making of such a large-scale and systematic comparison of delinquents and nondelinquents under conditions as nearly as possible approaching those of a scientific laboratory required much effort, patience, and ingenuity. How it was done is the subject of several lengthy chapters in *Unraveling Juvenile Delinquency*. Here we want merely to mention a few of the problems encountered along the path to accurate facts.

First, there was the task of finding a suitable place for carrying out the project. After some exploration we decided to select delinquent boys from among the population of two of the correctional schools of Massachusetts, and the nondelinquents from public schools in Boston.

Innumerable difficulties and details were involved in selecting and matching the boys, winning and keeping their cooperation and that of their parents, arranging for the many tests and examinations; and in assigning members of the staff to those portions of the inquiry in which they could do their most effective work.

Matching of the boys on the basis of four variables—age, general intelligence, ethnic derivation, and residence in underprivileged neighborhoods—entailed checking numerous details about many hundreds of boys, before a reliable pairing of 500 persistent delinquents and 500 true nondelinquents could be accomplished. To mention but one detail, freedom from delinquent behavior (the kind of conduct that brings boys to the attention of the police and the juvenile court) was determined not only by checkup of court files to ascertain the absence of official records, but also by special investigations of doubtful situations (inquiries among local police, social workers, recreational leaders, teachers, family physicians, and others in a position to know at first hand about a boy's acitivities, as well as from the psychiatrist's interview with each supposed nondelinquent).

The social investigations into the family and personal history of the boys involved consultation of innumerable records of public and private agencies; many interviews with parents, teachers, and others; the checking of court, correctional institution, and hospital records; the gathering of school data; and the verification of hundreds of items before the facts could be entered onto statistical schedules. As a reflection of what was involved in obtaining reliable data it may be pointed out that the inquiries into the family and personal history of the thousand boys, begun in the fall of 1940, were not finished until early in 1948.

Before any large-scale gathering of the vast materials could be undertaken, definitions, subcategories, and statistical schedules had to be tested; many safeguards had to be placed about the recording of the data; substantiating evidence for various findings had to be checked. When all the data had been assembled on a given case, the schedules had to be edited.

The editing of the completed schedules involved the collation of data from several sources. To cite one example, information on a boy's use of leisure was secured from parents, from reports of social workers who had dealt with the boy's family in the past or were actively interested, from correctional and school authorities, and from the psychiatrist's interview with the boy. All the observations and findings recorded in respect to this particular factor had to be weighed, and the final consolidation placed in its appropriate statistical category.

The size of the enterprise may be gleaned from the fact that the social investigation schedules comprised 149 items, the physique 55, the medical 30, the psychologic 56, the Rorschach Test 57, the psychiatric examination 55—making a grand total of 402 factors. The full story of this vast inquiry cannot be here recorded. The interested reader will find in *Unraveling Juvenile Delinquency* (Chapters II to VIII) a description of the design of the research and of its methodology. He will see that there is far more in the determination of a "fact" than meets the eye.

A pioneering social research is beset with many problems, both in its initial planning and in its execution, that are seemingly extraneous to the research itself, such, for example, as taking the time to explain the purpose of the inquiry and its possible ultimate social value to skeptical families, school and correctional officials, social workers, and others from whom data has to be secured; or, to counter difficulties and obstacles by building a reservoir of good will in the community, smoothing over misunderstandings, preventing injury to the sensibilities of the larger community by scrupulous avoidance of careless statements about the nature and purpose of the research; and so on.

We hope that even on the basis of this necessarily incomplete account of how the inquiry was planned and carried out the reader will turn with confidence to the findings that follow.

Before considering the findings en masse, it will stimulate interest to present the contrasting pictures of a delinquent and a nondelinquent and invite the reader to guess which is which.

CHAPTER III

Meet Frankie and Jimmy

Meet Frankie and Jimmy! They constitute one of the 500 matched pairs of persistent delinquents and true nondelinquents whom we describe in this book. We are not going to reveal until later whether it is Frankie or Jimmy who is the lawbreaker.

When we first encountered Frankie and Jimmy, the former was fourteen years and five months old, and the latter fourteen years and eight months. On the Wechsler-Bellevue intelligence test, Frankie has an intelligence quotient (I.Q.) of 98; Jimmy's is quite similar, being 106. (An I.Q. of 90-110 is usually taken to signify normal, or average, intelligence.)

Both boys are of Italian extraction and the parents of both were born in Italy. Frankie's mother and father had migrated to the United States almost twenty years before the boy was born; Jimmy's parents had not been in this country quite so long—about a dozen years.

Frankie's mother and father are living; Jimmy's father died when the boy was six months old.

Both lads are the youngest children in the family, Frankie being one of eight brothers and sisters, Jimmy the youngest of four.

In both their families there has been criminality, alcoholism, intellectual defect, and mental disorder.

Some of Frankie's relatives on his father's side had committed crimes which brought them into conflict with the legal authorities, and one sister and three brothers of his had been arrested on charges of larceny, robbery, lewdness, gambling. Several of them had also been persistent school truants. As a young woman, Frankie's mother had been convicted of petty stealing from a variety store.

One of Jimmy's brothers and a sister had likewise come into conflict with the legal authorities for offenses ranging from truancy to larceny. Jimmy's mother had once been placed on probation, but the offense was deemed to be of a minor nature. His father (who, you will remember, died when Jimmy was only six months old) had been a nonsupporter, and had been arrested for carrying a loaded revolver and for committing assault and battery on Jimmy's mother.

Nothing is known about alcoholism among the relatives of Frankie's father, but one of Frankie's brothers and one sister are confirmed alcoholics. Jimmy's father had been a heavy drinker.

Regarding physical health, we have learned that both a paternal and a maternal aunt of Frankie had suffered from pulmonary tuberculosis. Of the immediate family group, it is known that two of the boy's brothers died of pneumonia in infancy, one of his sisters is in "poor health," and the entire family are underweight. These facts have been verified by a welfare agency which has had to assist the family with food and funds over many years.

Nothing is known about the health of Jimmy's paternal and maternal relatives, but his father was a victim of rheumatism and of organic heart disease, his death being caused, at the age of thirty-seven, by the latter condition. Jimmy's mother also suffers from frequent rheumatic attacks.

As regards intellectual defect, two of Frankie's brothers and two of his sisters have intelligence quotients under 70 (feeble-mindedness is placed by psychologists below an I.Q. of 70), one of his sisters having an I.Q. as low as 56. Both of

Frankie's parents are definitely of low mentality, although their exact I.Q. has never been determined.

Nothing is known about the intelligence of Jimmy's father, but his mother has been reported by social agencies to be of average intelligence. However, one of his brothers and two of his sisters are so retarded that they had to be assigned to special classes in the schools.

We know little about the emotional distortions in the two families so far as concerns the boys' grandparents and great-aunts and -uncles. There is, however, some evidence of enduring emotional stress in Frankie's father, who is a severe stammerer, as is one of Frankie's brothers. His mother is "highstrung" and considers herself a "martyr." A child guidance clinic describes her as very "voluble" and a "complaining type." According to another competent social welfare agency, one of Frankie's sisters is extremely unmanageable, profane and "slack."

Jimmy's mother describes his long-deceased father as having been "irrational at times; he went crazy with drink." A welfare agency which had known him years ago reports that he had been in a mental hospital in Italy. Jimmy's mother is described by welfare and court workers as "crafty, hot-tempered, and high-strung."

What has been the intellectual-cultural heritage of the two boys?

Frankie's paternal grandparents were illiterates. We know nothing of the situation among his maternal relatives. Frankie's father attended school in Italy until the fourth grade; he can barely read and write Italian. His mother, who also was reared in Italy, is entirely illiterate.

Jimmy's grandparents all attended grade school and his paternal grandfather had had some high school education in Italy. Jimmy's father had likewise gone to high school, but his mother can neither read nor write.

Both the paternal and maternal grandparents of Frankie had tilled the soil in the old country, barely eking out a living. On the other hand, Jimmy's paternal grandfather had been an apothecary, his maternal grandfather a shoemaker. Extreme poverty had been the lot of Frankie's ancestors. Jimmy's more than managed to keep their heads above water.

At this stage of the comparison would you venture to say whether it is Frankie or Jimmy who is the persistent delinquent?

Both boys are, of course, living in the slums, more specifically in deteriorating tenement areas.

The neighborhood of Frankie's home is alive with exciting gang and street activities; there are dumps and empty lots, railroad yards and tracks, wharves and piers in the vicinity.

The neighborhood of Jimmy's home also is gang-ridden and bristling with street activities; there are alleyways and barrooms roundabout.

The opportunities for acquiring criminalistic habits and companions in this typical "delinquency area" were thus open to both youngsters.

Now we step from the street influences across the threshold into the homes of these lads.

Frankie's family, which, at present, consists of his father and mother, three brothers, and one sister, live on the top floor of a three-family tenement. They have eight rooms, for which they pay $30 a month. Frankie shares a room with a brother, but has his own bed. Except for the lack of central heating, all sanitary facilities are present.

Jimmy lives with his mother, one brother, and two sisters. They have four rooms, of which three are used as bedrooms, while a daybed converts the living room into sleeping quarters at night. Although in the past conditions were extremely crowded in this home, the four children having had to share one bed, at present Jimmy sleeps on the living-room daybed with his brother. As in Frankie's home, there is a bathroom, hot water, and electric light, but no central heating.

There is a sufficiency of furnishings in both homes, enough to meet the necessities; no extras and no luxuries.

Frankie's mother is a tidy housekeeper. She makes every effort to keep herself and the home neat and clean. Jimmy's mother likewise is a good housekeeper, although it cannot be said that she has always been such; at one time she was untidy and slovenly. It was not until Jimmy's sister left school, remaining at home to help her mother, that a considerable change for the better took place in the household management and routine.

Both families are poverty stricken. Frankie's just manages to keep its head above water; Jimmy's has been out-and-out dependent upon public and private welfare agencies since long before the boy was born.

Sixteen welfare agencies have provided help and advice to Frankie's immediate family, beginning even before his birth. Not only has financial propping been needed from time to time, but there have been numerous family problems arising from physical and mental ill-health, and from recreational and employment needs of one kind or another over the years, in which the skilled guidance of social workers has been needed.

Jimmy's family, too, have had to turn to welfare organizations, eleven agencies having had contact with the family, beginning even before his birth. Here financial dependence has been unbroken, because of the father's defections (he was a habitual drinker and gambler, to the point of its interfering with his ability to hold a job). Since his death when Jimmy was a baby, Jimmy's mother, who was left with young children, has had to have public support. Welfare agencies have given her advice and help on numerous problems having to do with matters of health, recreation, and employment.

Frankie's father, who has been an unskilled laborer, working usually in factories as a porter, is at present unemployed. His health was so poor by the time Frankie was twelve that he has not been able to work since; but Frankie's mother, sisters, and three brothers have jobs and between them they earn $75 a week, which makes an average income of $10.70 a week per person for this household.

In Jimmy's home, only one sister is working and then only part time. Of the $8 a week that she earns, she contributes $5.40 to the household. In addition to this, the money that is provided by a public welfare agency results in an average weekly income of $4.08 per person. Jimmy's mother somehow makes it do.

Again we pause to ask the reader whether the indications thus far permit him to decide which boy is the delinquent.

Let us now look into some personal aspects of what might be called the under-the-roof situation in the two homes.

The behavior standards in both households leave much to be desired. It should be recalled that Frankie's mother had been convicted of larceny and that one of his sisters and three of his brothers also had been in serious difficulty with the legal authorities. In Jimmy's home, also, the conduct standards have been far from good, as evidenced by the neglect of the family on the part of Jimmy's father, by the mother's delinquency as a girl, by the delinquencies of one of Jimmy's sisters and one of his brothers. A social agency has reported that Jimmy's mother encouraged him and the other children to "spit on neighbors' plants and to urinate from the window." Despite this, it was agreed that she is essentially "not vicious."

It can hardly be said that very much self-respect is present in either family. Frankie's kin accepted aid from public welfare agencies under false pretenses, even while some members of the family were working. Jimmy's were public charges even before the boy was born. But this has not completely demoralized them. Although it is clear that Jimmy's mother "knows all the ropes of charity," she nevertheless shows some pride and some desire to be independent of public support. However, in neither family is there any evidence of any ambition to improve their status other than the desire for a little more of the comforts of life. Nor have the members of either family given any thought to Frankie's or Jimmy's future. Apparently the boys will have to make their own way as best they can.

In neither circle is it customary for the members of the family to join in any group recreations, such as picnics, visits to relatives, attendance at the movies, enjoyment of a hobby, and the like. Every member of each family goes his or her own way in pursuit of pleasure.

Sometimes, when Frankie misconducts himself, his father and mother resort to "licking" him. More generally, however, they are lax in their discipline. Neither of them makes any great effort to control the boy. As Jimmy does not have a father, his discipline has been entirely in his mother's hands. She is more likely to resort to mild threats of physical punishment. In the past two years, since Jimmy's recovery from a severe attack of rheumatic fever, his mother has, "on doctor's orders," rarely even admonished him for fear that he might have a relapse.

In the homes of both Frankie and Jimmy, mother is definitely the "boss." She directs the affairs of the family, controlling the spending and to a large extent the activities of the children. Although Jimmy's father died when the boy was six months old, it is a fact that even long before the father's death Jimmy's mother held the reins.

What of the relationship of the boys' parents to each other?

Frankie's mother and father have never separated; their marriage has been described as "a love match." When we first encountered Frankie, his parents had already been married for twenty-three years and throughout this period had never been apart. Jimmy's parents had not fared so well. On occasions prior to the boy's birth, his father deserted his mother, to return, albeit briefly, to the family hearth. According to social agencies who knew them intimately in those days, Jimmy's parents bickered constantly.

Has the picture clarified yet? Is it Frankie or Jimmy who is the lawbreaker?

Let us look further into their homes for the answer.

Frankie's parents cling to their Italian customs. They speak practically no English. Possibly as a result of this, one of his brothers has developed a strong "anti-Italian" attitude.

In Jimmy's home his mother speaks English, albeit poorly; but she has taught all the children Italian. The children respect their mother's background and do not feel embarrassed by her foreign birth and by the occasional reversion to Italian customs. With the exception of one brother (mentally retarded and delinquent) who seems on the way to detaching himself from the family group, the family ties are close. Jimmy's married sister is a frequent visitor to the home.

How do the families compare in respect to affectional warmth and general concern of the parents for the boys?

Frankie's father has had little affection for him, and his mother's attitude is well reflected in a comment she made years ago to a social worker that "the children make me tired." She has often resented having to give up an outside job to look after them. Despite his mother's not too great affection or concern about him, Frankie is strongly attached to her. But he is quite indifferent to his father, whom he does not admire.

Jimmy has been deprived of his father since babyhood, but perhaps the warmth and deep concern of his mother for him makes up for this. One of Jimmy's sisters long ago expressed the feeling that "Jimmy is my mother's favorite" and that she overindulges him. Maybe this is because Jimmy, as a baby, had frequent colds and coughs and mild rickets and made very slow gains in weight; and maybe also because Jimmy's mother had been deprived of the normal love of a husband.

Are we yet in a position to tell which boy is the delinquent? The reader will, we believe, once more have to reserve a decision.

What do we know about Frankie and Jimmy as infants and young children? What about their health? Their physique? The quality of their intelligence? Their temperamental, emotional, and characterial make-up? Their school life? Their leisure-time activities? Their interests and ambitions?

First, let us see if their health history enables us to label one of these boys the delinquent, the other the nondelinquent.

Frankie weighed only six pounds at birth. As an infant he had measles, whooping cough and chicken pox, and at the age of three he suffered a mild attack of rheumatic fever. In this same year he was unfortunately badly burned about the stomach and back and had to be hospitalized. He was very much of a whiner and "crybaby." When only five, he drank lime (probably by accident), and hovered between life and death for several days. At present, however, except for a slight dermographia (an hysteric nervous condition of "skin writing," in which a reddish tracing appears and stays for some time if the skin is rubbed with a blunt pencil), and cyanosis (blueness of skin), Frankie can be regarded as in good health. The physical examination revealed no defects of any kind.

Jimmy, who tipped the scales at seven and a half pounds at birth, had frequent colds and coughs, and despite his normal weight when born, was very slow in gaining. When he was less than a year old, he already had a deficiency disease (mild rickets). Other than this, it was not until Jimmy was eight that he had his first illness, a slight attack of measles. When he was thirteen, however, he had a severe rheumatic fever, which kept him bedridden for some months. A recent physical examination of Jimmy has revealed some congestion in his chest and marked nearsightedness, an exaggerated "knee jerk," slight dermographia, slight cyanosis. On the whole, however, his health and nutrition are good.

Despite the closeness in their ages (Frankie is 14 years and 5 months, Jimmy 14 years and 8 months), Frankie is much smaller than Jimmy. He stands only a little over 5 feet 1 inch and weighs 90 pounds, while Jimmy is 5 feet 4½ inches tall and weighs 139 lbs.

Frankie, who is predominantly lean, has considerable muscularity of the face, neck, and shoulder regions of his body, despite a slenderness in his lower extremities. He is short, slender, thin, has so far failed to show signs of physical maturity comparable with his age, and there is a considerable amount of disproportion between different parts of his body. Jimmy, on the other hand, is of the more robust, athletic type, but his legs do not show the same muscularity that is evident in other parts of his body. He is much taller and heavier than Frankie, is physically mature for his years, and has strong bone-muscle development.

Perhaps some readers at last feel certain which one of these boys is the delinquent.

Let us see whether we can further clarify the picture from a consideration of their intellectual make-up.

It should be remembered that Frankie and Jimmy, like all the 500 pairs of delinquents and nondelinquents, were closely matched on the basis of their total intelligence quotients, Frankie's I. Q. being 98, Jimmy's 106. These totals represent the *averages* of Frankie's and Jimmy's scores on the verbal and performance components of the Wechsler-Bellevue Intelligence Test. Analyzing the *constituents* of the test, we find that in Frankie's case his performance score (or "hand-mindedness") is higher than his verbal ability (104:93). Jimmy, on the contrary, has a higher verbal than a performance score (112:98). Evidently Frankie learns largely through doing things with his hands, while Jimmy is the more intellectual of the two, absorbing knowledge more readily through symbols.

This difference in the quality of their intelligence is clearly reflected in the school history of the two boys: when we first encountered Frankie, he was in the fifth grade, while Jimmy at the same age was already in the ninth. Frankie lagged three years behind the grade appropriate to his age. He was also very much behind in reading (his reading quotient being 74, as compared with Jimmy's 113). School achievement tests in arithmetic also show him to be behind Jimmy (67:86).

What have we learned about the difference in the quality of the intelligence of these two boys? Through the Rorschach Test we found that Frankie is lacking in good powers of observation, while Jimmy has them. Frankie lacks ability to think realistically, while Jimmy is able to do so. Frankie is short on "common sense," while Jimmy has it in marked degree. Frankie tends to slip into the make-believe land of fantasy; Jimmy has his mental feet square on the ground. Frankie is not able to approach problems methodically; Jimmy is. Certainly, there is a marked difference between these two boys in the *components* of their intellectual make-up, although both rate "normal" in intelligence quotient.

We wonder whether the reader is yet able to say with assurance which of the two boys is the juvenile delinquent.

Perhaps further clues will provide a conclusive answer.

What of their temperamental traits, as evident to a skilled psychiatrist?

Frankie was found to be an extrovert, both in action and in feeling (which means that he expresses himself without inhibition in conduct and emotions). He is highly suggestible, that is, easily swayed by an appeal to his feelings, even though against his better judgment. He is acquisitive, being inclined to acquire material things over and above any desire, or any immediate need, for them. He is adventuresome, that is, he has a strong impulse toward change, excitement, risk-taking.

Jimmy, on the other hand, is "adequate," that is, he is able to conduct and express himself with a fair degree of efficiency. He is emotionally stable. He is sensitive, that is, he has an acute awareness of situations and stimuli and their implications, and has developed suitable inhibitions for coping with them. Unlike Frankie, Jimmy is inclined to follow an accepted social code. He is conventional (following the safe and familiar courses of conduct).

From the Rorschach ("ink-blot") Test, much was learned about the deeply embedded character structure of Frankie and Jimmy. Frankie is inclined to give expression to his will and his ambitions. In other words, he is "socially assertive." He is also defiant, destructive, and has a great inner need for power, superiority, and status. Psychiatrists would describe him as "narcissistic." Yet, Frankie does not suffer from feelings of insecurity, anxiety, inferiority, and frustration.

Jimmy, on the other hand, is markedly submissive to both authority and society. By this he gains a feeling of security, first in relation to his mother, and then to others. He fears public opinion and is inclined to conventional attitudes and behavior. Despite his mother's manifest devotion to him, Jimmy has a strong inner feeling of not being wanted or loved. The Rorschach analyst points out that such a feeling is "very often repressed, has become unconscious, and tends to an exaggerated need for affection, recognition, success." Jimmy also reveals an attitude of "not being taken seriously" or "not counting," which leads to a feeling of "helplessness and powerlessness," from which Jimmy clearly suffers. According to the Rorschach analyst, Jimmy was evidently made to feel in early childhood, perhaps inadvertently, that whatever he did was only "child's play" and that whatever did not coincide with the wishes and ideas of his mother deserved no serious consideration in its own right. It is not surprising to find, then, that Jimmy grew up with a strong fear of failure and defeat, which is a frequent consequence of anxiety. In Jimmy was also unearthed a tendency to suffer and to be dependent. Psychiatrists call it "masochism."

The basic differences in the personality and characteral structures of Frankie and Jimmy must already be clear to the reader.

What else did the Rorschach probing reveal about the differences in the internal emotional-dynamic make-up of these two lads?

Frankie emerges as an extremely hostile person. He has deep-seated impulses of unfriendliness toward others without a normal reason for them. The Rorschach analyst points out that "usually this goes together with the feeling or fear that others are hostile toward oneself." Jimmy, on the other hand, though indiscriminately suspicious of others, nevertheless makes good contacts with people and is cooperative. At least on the surface he is able to get along with others.

Regarding certain more pervasive dynamics of personality, there are again marked differences between Frankie and Jimmy. Frankie is very impulsive. He discharges his feelings vehemently, without much control, working them off in emotional outbursts, or "explosions" (temper tantrums). He is outgoing, an extrovert, and manifests a liveliness of behavior often found in such persons.

Jimmy, on the other hand, is self-controlled; he is quite the opposite of Frankie in regard to impulsiveness, for he has the ability to hold back and canalize the discharge of his feelings into harmless channels.

As regards the emotional dependence of the boys on other people, Frankie is certainly not a dependent personality. True, he is suggestible in the sense that he has few inhibitions and makes little deliberate realistic and logical evaluation of a situation. But this suggestibility is "negative" in that his emotional drives lead him typically to hostile opposition to any attempts to persuade him to comply with authority. Jimmy, on the other hand, is very dependent on other people and he is eager to meet their expectations of him.

Frankie can be characterized as irresponsible, flighty, unreliable; he lacks any sense of self-discipline, self-control, persistence. This may partially account for the fact that despite his native intellectual endowment his achievements are far below his capacities.

In summary, the Rorschach analyst found that Frankie has grandiose notions about himself, and ideas of adventure and ambition which are entirely unrealistic; he would like to have everything; he has strong wishes and impulses and is unable to control them for any length of time; he has a marked hostility to others, especially to authoritative adults, whom he fears and distrusts. His labile emotional tendency soon overcomes whatever caution and hesitancy he may be able to muster, and he quickly becomes involved in irresponsible behavior. All in all, says the Rorschach expert, "he is a psychopathic type with some neurotic tendencies."

In contrast, Jimmy "tries to meet the expectations of authoritative adults and has accepted and internalized their commands and taboos." He is often fearful that he will not be able to meet all their demands and expectations and he therefore tries to anticipate their wishes. This he does because internally he is under rather strong "authoritative pressure" (or governed by a rigid conscience) and is therefore not free to think or act spontaneously. Situations which call for spontaneity or an appeal to his emotions threaten to upset him and he unconsciously responds to this threat by tightening his control on himself and becoming more and more inhibited. The Rorschach analyst concludes that he is "a quite normal though unfree and somewhat inhibited boy, with some neurotic trends."

By now the picture should be clear.

It is Frankie and not Jimmy who is the juvenile delinquent!
How early in their lives did this become evident?

Frankie began to be troublesome even in the first grade of school, and soon began to truant. He engaged in pranks, was pugnacious, was constantly "fooling" in class, and even in the earliest years had a general appearance of "sloppiness." His various teachers have described him as untruthful, unreliable, untrustworthy, "a cheat;" impertinent, impudent, cruel; lazy, disorderly, careless, inattentive, stubborn; sullen, thoughtless, making much effort to attract attention, interrupting frequently, whispering—altogether "a terror." On one occasion, when he was eleven, Frankie was expelled from school for a brief period. His most recent teacher describes him as "more mature" (in the ways of the world) than the rest of his classmates, who, by the way, "did not bother with him." Frankie prefers an older boy as a companion.

Jimmy, on the other hand, established a consistently good conduct record in school. His teachers say that he "seemed at ease" with his classmates; that he has not been a "problem;" that his outstanding characteristic is "a desire to do as others do and to be well-thought-of by his associates."

Frankie has shown a distinctly resistant attitude toward school, while Jimmy, in contrast, has always readily accepted school. Frankie has expressed violent dislikes for arithmetic and geography, but Jimmy has no strong aversions.

Despite whippings from his parents, Frankie often stayed away from school in the hope of being transferred to another school where there were a lot of "fresh kids" and where the program, which included woodworking and other manual arts, was much more to his liking than were reading, writing, and arithmetic.

Frankie, who has not gone beyond the fifth grade, has no educational or vocational ambitions. He certainly does not intend to continue with his schooling. Jimmy, on the other hand, who has attained the ninth grade, wants to complete high school and become a machinist.

Both boys have worked after school, Frankie on weekends in a street trade (shining shoes); Jimmy during one summer vacation as a mason's helper. Frankie's primary reason for working has been to earn money for himself without regard for the needs of his family, to whom he has not offered any of it. Jimmy's purpose in working has been largely to help his mother with her scanty finances and to have a little spending money for himself. Frankie was very careless in the spending of his money; Jimmy spent most planfully what little he was given or earned.

What did these two boys usually do in their spare time?

Frankie, from his earliest years, has run about unbridled in the streets, usually rather far away from his home. When only five he began to indulge in destructive play with a companion somewhat older than himself, largely breaking windows "for excitement." At six he started to truant from school with another boy. He recalls "having fun" catching fish and crabs and cooking them at the beach. At other times he and his special pal would "hop" on streetcars. To this exciting activity he was greatly devoted.

Frankie further recalls that when he was six years old he "swiped" four wheels from a baby carriage parked near his house. This he did in the company of another boy who was older than himself and already a confirmed delinquent.

Frankie soon became adept at stealing toy popguns from the variety stores for the use of his "gang," who had grown tired of playing cops and robbers with wooden guns.

At about the age of six Frankie was introduced by a somewhat older boy to sex play with other boys.

When he was seven years old he was accused by a little girl of attempting to attack her with a jackknife; although the police were called, Frankie was not taken to court. In frequent truck-hopping expeditions, always in the company of another boy, he would steal chocolates, pickles, eggs, and tennis sneakers. This was soon extended to "clipping" sweets from candy shops, a practice in which his gang indulged without fear of punishment. It was not long before Frankie became more ambitious in his thefts and with one of his older companions began to steal from parked automobiles any objects that appealed to him. *At this time he was barely eight.*

Though he had already come to the attention of the police on several occasions and had been apprehended (the first time when he was five), he was quickly released. But in his eighth year his formal criminal record began, for "larceny of tonic." With some ten members of his gang he had two months previously begun to "swipe" soft drinks from a truck; and one day, while the truck was parked in front of a local store, the driver seized several of the boys and the police were called. Since that occasion he has been arrested eight times for breaking, entering, and larceny; for willful injury to property; for stealing rides; for attempts to commit assault and battery.

Frankie boasts that, despite the fact that the police have been closely on his trail during these years, many of his "greatest crimes" are unknown to them.

Meanwhile, Jimmy, too, had been growing up in a crowded slum neighborhood. But unlike Frankie he rarely played on the streets. His mother complains that he still spends too much time at home, reading. From his earliest years Jimmy has had few friends. They have been both boys and girls of his own age; and certainly not delinquents. When asked by the psychiatrist why he has not fallen a prey to the temptations to steal, he says: "I'd be scared to death to do it."

Both boys attend settlement houses in the neighborhood; but Frankie does so at the behest of a probation officer, and is quite indifferent to the club activities, attending only once a week to see a movie. Jimmy, on the other hand, has joined two clubs entirely of his own volition. He goes there almost daily for athletics, and often uses the library. He is most enthusiastic about his club activities and does not have to be coaxed to attend.

The background, make-up, and activities of Frankie and Jimmy have been presented. The reader's hindsight may cause him to think that he knew from the first few facts that it is Frankie who is causing trouble to society; but if he retraces his steps he will have to admit that there are many elements in the lives of Frankie and Jimmy that run counter to the accepted notions of the causes of crime.

Since there are numerous aspects of Frankie's and Jimmy's life which might make it appear that Frankie is the nondelinquent rather than the lawbreaker, and that Jimmy is the delinquent, we hope that many questions have been raised in the reader's mind regarding his own concepts of the causes of juvenile delinquency. Obviously it is only from a study of hundreds of boys in the mass and at various levels of inquiry that we can get closer to answers to the riddle of delinquency. It is for this reason that we have compared 500 delinquents with 500 nondelinquents.

CHAPTER IV

Family Wellsprings[1]

How typical of juvenile offenders is the Frankie of the previous chapter? And how typical is Jimmy of boys growing up in the slums of our large cities who do not resort to antisocial behavior despite the deprivations and pressures of a vicious environment? Some light may be thrown on this question by turning to a comparison of the 500 young delinquents and their 500 match-mates, all living in underprivileged urban areas.

These are regions of considerable physical and moral deterioration and delinquency.[2] They are usually adjacent to areas of industry and commerce; the houses they contain are dilapidated, the rents low; there are dirty alleys; there is much dependence and poverty. Both groups of boys compared in this study were selected from such areas, as evidenced by the closeness of the incidence of delinquency

[1] Ten investigators were occupied for varying periods between 1940 and 1948 in reconstructing the family and personal histories of the 500 delinquents and 500 nondelinquents. Three were associated with the project throughout: Mildred Pilpel Cunningham, George F. McGrath, and Ava E. Burrows.

[2] Clifford R. Shaw, in *Delinquency Areas* (University of Chicago Press, 1929), pp. 203, 204, points out that "High [delinquency] rates occur in the areas which are characterized by physical deterioration and declining populations. . . The areas in which the greatest concentrations and highest rates are found have many characteristics which differentiate them from the outlying residential communities . . . These areas are in a process of transition from residence to business and industry, and are characterized by physical deterioration, decreasing population, and the disintegration of the conventional neighborhood culture and organizations."

rates: 59% of the delinquents and 54% of the nondelinquents lived in neighborhoods in which the delinquency
rate was 10-24.9 per thousand; 20% of the former and
22% of the latter came from regions in which the delinquency rate was 25-49.9 per thousand; 15% of the antisocial boys and 17% of the other lads resided in areas in
which the delinquency rate was 50-100 per thousand. (See
Unraveling Juvenile Delinquency, p. 36, Table IV-2.)

The 500 delinquents whom we are about to describe averaged 14 years and 8 months, the nondelinquents 14 years
and 6 months, at the time they were taken on for study.
The age range was 11 to 17. In ethnic origin, a fourth of both
groups are of English background, a fourth are Italian, a
fifth are Irish. Less than a tenth are old American, or Slavic,
or French; and smaller percentages are Near Eastern in
origin, Portuguese, Spanish, Scandinavian, German, or
Jewish.

In intelligence, as measured by the Wechsler-Bellevue
Test, the delinquents average 92 in I.Q., the nondelinquents
94. Only a few of each group had intelligence quotients
either under 70 or over 120.

The Homes in which the Parents Were Reared

If it be true that "the apple does not fall far from the tree,"
then the first question to which we must direct our attention
concerns the background of the parents of our boys. From
what kind of people did they spring? In what kind of
environment were they reared? Since they must have carried
into the process of child care and discipline the ideational,
emotional, spiritual, and behavioral residues of their own
upbringing, it is relevant to consider some of the influences
to which these parents had been subjected. Their own childhood deprivations, frustrations, and other emotional erup-

tions and disruptions may well have been reflected in their attitudes and practices when they, in turn, had to deal with their children.

Some differences in the cultural environment, or what we shall call the *under-the-roof culture,* will become apparent and assume special significance for the very reason that the boys were originally matched on the basis of ethnic origin (Italian delinquent with Italian nondelinquent, Irish with Irish, and the like).

In respect to some matters, the families from which the parents came did not vary much: There was little difference in their size, and not much difference in the economic circumstances of the homes in which the two sets of parents had been reared. Almost without exception they lived in conditions of poverty or near poverty. Both sets of parents had been reared by fathers and mothers who had had little if any formal schooling.

More important is the burden of serious physical ailments, defective intelligence, emotional disturbances, drunkenness, and criminalism among the members of the parental families.[3]

In seeking evidence of serious physical ailments among the families of the parents of both groups of boys, we concentrated on the more severe diseases, such as cancer, tuberculosis, diabetes, disorders of the cardiovascular system and renal system; arthritis, syphilis, certain glandular disturbances, and diseases of the nervous system. Here again,

[3] In this area complete data were impossible to secure because records pertaining to the older generation were not kept as adequately by mental hospitals, courts, and social agencies as are those of more recent years, and because the data obtainable regarding relatives born and reared abroad were not sufficiently reliable for our purposes. We did not necessarily seek information about every member of a family group, but we did make a determined effort to search for positive evidence of the presence of serious physical and mental disturbances in at least one member.

The intensity and extent of the quest for such family data were the same for the nondelinquents as for the delinquents.

however, little difference emerged between the two sets of families: One or another of these ailments was found to have existed in varied combinations in over half the families of the fathers and the mothers of both the delinquent boys and the nondelinquents.

As regards defective intelligence among the families from which the parents of our boys sprang (not merely outright feeble-mindedness but also varying degrees of reported mental "dullness"), such a condition was definitely present in about a tenth of both delinquents' and nondelinquents' paternal families; however, the incidence of mental backwardness was one in four among the delinquents' maternal families, and only one in seven among the nondelinquents'.

More significant are the findings in respect to severe emotional disturbances—psychoses, psychopathies, psychoneuroses, epilepsies, sex inversions, marked emotional instability, and pronounced temperamental deviations. Long and patient search revealed that such conditions were present among one or more members of at least a fourth of the families from which the delinquents' fathers sprang, as compared with less than a fifth of the paternal families of the nondelinquents. The maternal families of the delinquents were also far more burdened with emotional disturbances than were those of the nondelinquents, the proportionate incidence being four to two.

Regarding chronic alcoholism among members of the paternal and maternal families, about a third of the fathers of both sets of boys had been reared in families in which one or more members were reported to have drunk to the point of intoxication, but almost half the mothers of delinquents, compared to about a third of the mothers of the nondelinquents, had grown up in such homes.

Criminalistic activities, also, flourished among the families in which the parents of our youngsters had been reared.

They were definitely more prevalent in the homes of the delinquents' parents and considerably more so in the households of the boys' mothers than in the paternal families. Four out of every ten of the fathers of our delinquents had their start in life in homes in which one or more of the immediate family group were delinquents or criminals, a proportion comparing with three in ten of the nondelinquents' fathers. Over half the maternal families of the former contained one or more criminalistic members, as contrasted with a third of the nondelinquents'.

It would seem obvious that fathers and mothers who themselves had been reared in an atmosphere of poverty combined with intellectual and educational inferiority, physical and mental disease, alcoholism and criminalism would not be likely to bring to the task of child rearing the intelligence, the solid moral standards, the ethical and religious ideals, and the peace of mind so indispensable to the wholesome emotional and intellectual rearing of youngsters, especially in the highly competitive, predatory, and generally exciting environment of the underprivileged urban area.

Moreover, it is of special significance for the destiny of the boys we have studied that their mothers came, on the whole, from even more undesirable families and more sordid homes than those which cradled their fathers.

Adequacy of Mothers and Fathers for Family Responsibilities

How adequate were the parents of the delinquents and nondelinquents for marriage and parenthood? It is this which, in large measure, was likely to determine the attitudes and behavior of the children whom they brought into the world.

Before taking up the factors in respect to which the

delinquents' parents were less adequate than those of the nondelinquents, we may dispose briefly of the factors regarding which there was little if any difference.

First about their education. The parents of both groups of boys had very little schooling—two in ten being wholly illiterate, five in ten having had no more than grammar school education.

They resembled each other also in age at marriage, half the mothers of both delinquents and nondelinquents having been under twenty-one at the time.

We turn now to differences between the parents of the two sets of boys.

First, it was found that four out of ten of the marriages of the parents of the delinquents, compared to three in ten of those of the nondelinquents, were "forced." Unexpected and unwanted propulsion into the marital status because of illegitimate pregnancy can hardly be regarded, even in these days of changing sex mores, as an auspicious beginning to the assumption of family responsibilities.

Secondly, a far higher proportion of the mothers of the delinquents than of the nondelinquents suffered from serious physical ailments, from intellectual retardation, from emotional disturbances, from drunkenness; and during their girlhood or later years, an excessive proportion of the delinquents' mothers had committed offenses which society labels delinquent or criminal. Similarly, the fathers of the delinquents were more burdened with physical, intellectual, emotional, and behavioral disturbances than were the fathers of the law-abiding boys.

Can it be doubted that such an array of handicaps to wholesome and intelligent parenthood leaves a deposit in the hearts and minds of children?

But that is not all.

In coping with poverty and dependence, which burdened

both sets of families, the greater inability of the parents of the delinquents to fulfill their family obligations is also strikingly evident. Eight out of ten of these families, compared with less than six in ten of the nondelinquents' families, were dependent on relief agencies or relatives for financial aid.

Moreover, apart from the equal proportion of families (one in seven) in which the chief reason for financial help was the physical or mental illness of the breadwinner, unwillingness of the breadwinner to assume his responsibilities was the main cause for resort to outside aid in the families of the delinquents, while inadequacy of income stemming from economic depression and seasonal unemployment accounted for need of financial assistance in the other families.

And all this assumes greater significance in the light of the fact that there was little difference among the two groups in the nature of the occupations of the principal breadwinners.[4]

In work habits, however, there is a considerable difference. Only half as many of the fathers of the delinquent group as of the nondelinquent could be characterized as having *good* work habits (i. e., as being an asset to employers; a reliable and good workman). At the other extreme, five time the proportion of the fathers in the delinquent group as in the nondelinquent were generally *poor* workers (i. e., inclined to loafing, laziness, lack of interest, waywardness, vagabondage, instability). A considerable portion of the fathers of the delinquents could be regarded as only *fair* workers (with the qualifications that might make them assets to their employers but inclined to permit their work to be interrupted by periodic drinking, occasional vagabondage, or deliberate choice of seasonal occupations).

The extent to which the parents of the delinquents were

[4] Few of the fathers were engaged in a business of their own, in clerical jobs, or in such public utility services as motormen, mailmen, and the like. A third were unskilled laborers; a tenth were truck drivers or teamsters; less than a third had skilled or semiskilled trades.

unable to fulfill their family obligations without outside help is further reflected in the fact that the average number of social welfare agencies that had to step in to serve the families of the delinquents in one way or another was twelve, a figure almost double that of the mean number of agencies serving the families of the nondelinquents. The types of service rendered ran almost the entire gamut of social work; and the families of the delinquents invariably required much more bolstering up than did those from which the nondelinquents came. The seriousness of the family problems can be implied from the fact that four of every five of the delinquents' families, compared to one in two of the nondelinquents', required some help toward solution of domestic difficulties and in situations originating from neglect and abuse of the children.

Inability to meet the family's needs by the parents' own resources is further reflected in the high proportions of both groups which had to have free or partially free hospital or clinical care or the services of public health agencies or visiting nurses. So, too, as regards services from agencies concerned with problems of mental health, a lesser ability is shown on the part of the delinquents' families to cope with their problems, as well as a greater incidence of outside aid. The high proportion of seven out of every ten of the former, compared to but two in ten of the nondelinquents' families, turned to psychiatric clinics, mental hospitals, schools for the feeble-minded, and similar agencies for help in meeting the mental problems of one or another member of the immediate family group.

The foregoing analysis makes it clear that despite such similarities in the two groups under comparison as size of parental families, depressed economic circumstances, limited parental education, and incidence of serious physical ailments in the family group, there are undoubted differences in the composition of the wellsprings of the two sets of families.

The paternal and maternal families of the delinquents were more extensively characterized by mental retardation, emotional disturbance, drunkenness, and criminalism. Whether these undesirable conditions are to be regarded as largely hereditary or largely environmental in origin is impossible to determine; but they must certainly have had their adverse influences upon the parents of our boys who, in their turn, had to assume the responsibilities of marriage and the care of their offspring.

The qualitative difference in the immediate families is strikingly revealed by the fact that unforeseeable conditions, such as economic depression and seasonal unemployment, were the bases of the need for financial aid among the largest proportion of the families of the nondelinquents, while, in the delinquents' families, unwillingness of the principal breadwinner to assume responsibility for support of the family was the chief reason for outside monetary aid. A further difference in the quality of the two sets of parents is reflected in the far lower proportion of fathers of the delinquents having good work habits.

By these simple yet fundamental measures, it is clear that the families into which the delinquents were born were more inadequate than those in which the nondelinquents were cradled.

Even this partial sampling of the wellsprings of the two sets of families shows that, while both familial streams were polluted, those which nurtured the delinquents were more so than were those which nourished the nondelinquents.

Further indications of the marked difference in the family milieu in which the two sets of boys grew to manhood is presented in the next chapter.

CHAPTER V

More About the Family

Continuing the analysis of the family milieu in which the delinquents and nondelinquents grew up, we focus on some of the more subtle aspects of family life than were revealed in the prior chapter. Here we are concerned with the orderliness of the households, the cultural refinement of the homes; family pride, self-respect, and ambitiousness; conduct standards; relationship between the parents; the mother's assumption of her responsibility to supervise her children; recreational outlets of the family, provisions for entertaining the children's friends at home; and, finally, the cohesiveness of the family group.

Orderliness of Household

First, as regards the orderliness of the households, much is reflected in the management of the family's income and in the routine of household activities. Inquiries into budgeting of income for food, rent, medical care, insurance, allowances for the children, installment purchasing and savings, established that there is less planfulness in the management of the family income in the households of the delinquents than in those of the other boys. As a group, the families of the delinquents were far more inclined to live from day to day, borrowing without thought of their ability to make reimbursement, and showing little comprehension of the value of limiting their expenditures to conform to a meager income.

As regards the routine established for the conduct of the household, the families of the nondelinquent boys more generally made an effort to avoid confusion in their daily living as reflected in a systematic concern with specific mealtimes and bedtimes for the children, hours for doing home lessons, and the like. Almost twice as many families of the delinquents as of the nondelinquents were completely slipshod in their way of life.

CULTURAL REFINEMENT OF HOME.   In exploring the home background of both delinquents and nondelinquents we sought evidence of appreciation of "the finer things of life," as reflected by love of music, art, literature, aesthetic home furnishings, and the like. Since the socioeconomic level of all the homes was low, there existed little opportunity for obtaining the means of aesthetic enjoyment. Nevertheless, even the poorest of families can assemble bits of the symbols of refinement. In most of the homes of the delinquents (nine in ten) and of the nondelinquents (eight in ten), there was complete lack of any evidence of aesthetic appreciation. In several instances one or two members of a family played musical instruments and were encouraged to do so by the elders in the household. But in only three homes of the delinquents and two of the nondelinquents was there marked refinement of taste reflected either in home decoration or in cultural interests. This is a finding that should attract the attention of schoolteachers, social workers, artists, and those interested in community organization.

Family Pride

In a further search for possible differences in the quality of the home life in which the delinquents and the nondelinquents were reared, we sought to determine the sense of responsibility and ambitiousness of the families as revealed in the attitude of the elders toward protecting the family name or in their embarrassment over any irregularity in the behavior and status of any members of the family group, and in their preference for self-help as opposed to outside sources for financial assistance. Here as in other aspects of the under-the-roof culture, we found that a much higher proportion of the families of the delinquents—four in ten—in contrast with but one in ten of the families of the nondelinquents, were definitely lacking in such attributes of self-respect.

Concerning the ambitiousness of the families, we sought evidence of a desire on the part of the parents for improvement in their status, as reflected in wanting higher education for their children; or in a serious intention to move to better neighborhoods in order to remove the children from economically and morally blighted regions; or in saving to buy a house so that the living conditions of the family might be stabilized; or in plans to establish a small business with a view to improving the family's economic status.

What we discovered is that by far the majority of both groups of families, but substantially more of the families of the delinquents (nine in ten, as compared with seven in ten) gave no thought to the future, while only one in ten of the families of the delinquents, in contrast to nearly three in ten of those of the nondelinquents, showed some desire to improve their status.

Conduct Standards of Home

Examining, next, the conduct standards of the homes in which the boys were reared, we again find a marked contrast between the families of the delinquents and those of the nondelinquents. To determine behavior standards, we sought evidences of immorality, alcoholism, and criminality among the family members. It is already clear from the previous chapter that these conditions were found to exist among a considerably higher proportion of the mothers and fathers and brothers and sisters of the delinquents than of the nondelinquents. Viewing each family as a unit on the basis of all available objective evidence, we found that the conduct standards of the homes in which the delinquents grew up were far worse than those which prevailed in the homes of the nondelinquents, the standards being definable as low in nine out of ten of the former compared to five out of ten of the latter.

Relationship of Parents

Since it is the parents who set the tenor of the family life, and by their relationship to each other determine the affectional mood of the home, it is crucially important to learn something about the quality of their feeling for each other. The relationship of only a third of the parents of the delinquents compared to two-thirds of the parents of the nondelinquents could be considered *good,* by which we mean that they were living together in harmony. In another third of the families of the delinquents and in a fifth of those of the nondelinquents, the parents were in fact not compatible, but no open breach had occurred between them except possibly an occasional separation followed by a reunion. But in one in three of the families of the delinquents, as compared with only one in seven of the nondelinquents', the inharmonious relationship of the parents had already resulted in an open breach, one or the other parent having left or deserted the family. The disastrous effect on children of incompatibility of parents need not be labored.

Mother as Head of the Household

Much has been written in recent years about the dominant position of the mother in the American household. The families we have studied appear to follow the prevalent pattern in this regard, for there is no difference in the status of the mothers of delinquents and nondelinquents in the extent to which they, rather than the fathers of the boys, guided the affairs of the family. In five among ten of the families of both groups, the mother was the obvious head, assuming in considerable measure the direction of the family life—disciplining the children, controlling expenditures, and managing the household affairs.

Although in equal proportion the homes in which the delinquents and nondelinquents grew up were mother-dominated, this does not mean that the mothers fulfilled their obligations to the children in equal measure. Many more of the delinquent boys were deprived of maternal supervision. This may be explained by the fact that a greater proportion of such mothers worked outside the home in jobs which undoubtedly absorbed most of their energies—domestic service by the hour or day, factory work, cleaning and scrubbing offices, running stores and lodging houses, and as waitresses in cafés and restaurants. The necessity for the mothers to work was of course partly due to the low economic status of the families; but it must be remembered that inadequacy of income characterized the families of the nondelinquents as well. It may therefore be that a considerable portion of this out-of-the-home labor on the part of the delinquents' mothers was motivated by a desire to escape from the confinement and responsibilities of their drab and burdensome households.

As might be expected, a much lower proportion of the mothers of the delinquents (less than one in ten as compared with almost seven in ten of the mothers of the nondelinquents) either gave or arranged suitable supervision for the boys. Many more of the mothers of the delinquents left their children to shift for themselves or placed them in the care of an irresponsible child or adult.

Objective evidence of the resultant laxity in supervision of the children is found in the fact that three in ten of the delinquent boys, as compared with a mere handful of the nondelinquents, were street beggars. Although there are obviously many other circumstances that lead to begging, so marked a difference between the delinquents and the nondelinquents must, in part at least, be attributed to poor parental supervision.

Certainly maternal neglect and careless oversight of children are generally recognized as major sources of maladaptation and delinquency, and clearly the mothers of the delinquent boys as a group were far more remiss in the care of their children than were the mothers of the nondelinquents.

Recreational Outlets of Family

Not only was there less supervision of the delinquent boys, but there was also less provision for recreational activities for the family as a group, such as picnicking or going to the beach together, auto riding, visiting relatives, or attending the movies together. Group recreations were not at all customary among two-thirds of the families of the delinquents in contrast to a third of the others. In only eleven of the entire five hundred families of the delinquents, as compared with some fifty of the families of the nondelinquents were group recreations entirely customary.

Failure of the parents to foster recreational outlets in which all members of the family participated certainly reflects the lesser cohesion of the families of the delinquents. Such neglect of an opportunity to develop family solidarity and a commonality of interests must tend to increase the likelihood of conduct which reflects little or no regard for family desires or standards or pride.

The reliance of the delinquent boys upon their own devices for their frequently antisocial recreational outlets was further aggravated by the failure of their parents to give any serious thought to making the homes attractive enough to encourage the children to bring in their playmates. Only two in ten of the families of the delinquents were hospitable to their children's friends, as compared with four in ten of the nondelinquents' families.

Small wonder, then, that the homes of most of the delinquents were not places which the children enjoyed. The reader will see in a later chapter how much time the delinquent boys spent in the streets and with gangs, an understandable reaction to the unattractiveness and inhospitality of their homes.

Not only were the families of the delinquent boys less hospitable to their children's friends, but they also provided less means for the wholesome enjoyment of the leisure hours of their children. In over half the homes of the delinquents as compared with a third of the homes of the other boys, recreational facilities were meager, consisting of only an occasional book or toy. In almost another half of the families in both groups there was a radio and a few games, and perhaps books were provided, but even this could hardly be considered sufficient enticement from the competition of exciting street activities. In only twenty of the five hundred families of the delinquents, as compared with sixty-nine of the other families, were diversified recreational facilities provided, such as games, books, perhaps a musical instrument or two, and material for hobbies.

Fewer recreational facilities in their homes may partially explain the lower proportion of delinquents who had hobbies, such as raising pigeons, building airplane models, collecting stamps, (one in ten of the delinquents, as compared with three in ten of the nondelinquents).

Cohesiveness of Family

There is already considerable evidence that the forces of disruption in the families of the delinquents were greater than those making for cohesion. A far lower proportion of such families than of those of the nondelinquents evinced strong affectional ties among the members, shared joint interests, took pride in their homes, and felt themselves to be "one for all and all for one." Such a pervasive attitude of solidarity was found in less than two in ten of the families of the delinquents, as compared with six in ten of the families of the nondelinquents. Thus, in the highly important quality that is both expressive of loyalty to the blood group and supportive of the individual in his sense of security and devotion to others, the delinquents were far more deprived than the nondelinquents.

The reader must by now fully appreciate the poorer quality of the family life of the delinquents. There was less effective household management and routine and less refinement of cultural atmosphere. Parents were less self-respecting than those of the nondelinquents and less ambitious to improve their social and economic status or that of their children. Standards of conduct were likewise much lower in the homes in which the delinquents grew up.

Nor was the quality of the family life of the delinquents as good as that of the nondelinquents in aspects more intimately related to child welfare. This is so in regard to the relationship between the parents, the supervision of the children, provision for recreation in or outside the home, and finally in the closeness of family ties.

Can there be any doubt that the human environment in which the delinquent boys grew up was less conducive to the rearing of wholesome, happy, and law-abiding children than that in which the nondelinquent boys were reared?

Since the two sets of youngsters had been carefully matched at the outset, not only in respect to age and general intelligence (factors involving only the boys themselves) but also with reference to ethnic-racial derivation and residence in underprivileged neighborhoods, the differences between the families of the delinquents and those of the nondelinquents which have emerged in this and other portions of the inquiry are all the more significant.

Many a reader will conclude that the poorer quality of family life, parental standards and behavior are in themselves sufficient to account for the dismal destiny of the delinquent children. But once more we must ask that judgment be deferred, for quite a number of the nondelinquent boys were reared under equally unfavorable conditions.

Let us therefore wait until all the threads of the tangled skein woven by nature and nurture are more clearly laid out, before we seek to reweave them into a meaningful pattern of cause-and-effect.

CHAPTER VI

The Boy at Home

We turn now to the dynamics of the home environment, focusing attention on those elements which directly affected the delinquent and the nondelinquent boys. What of their birth and early development, their growth and vicissitudes within the family group, the changes in the make-up of the households of which they were a part, the affectional relations between them and their parents and their brothers and sisters? What of the concern of the parents for the welfare of the boys? What of the extent to which the youngsters felt that their fathers were suitable objects for admiration and emulation? Finally, what of the ways in which the parents sought to discipline the boys for their misdoings?

Some Vital Statistics

Before assessing these important matters, it will be of help to consider several basic vital statistics: First, almost two in ten of the delinquents and one in ten of the nondelinquents had been conceived out of wedlock. In this connection it should be noted that the parents of thirty-one of the 500 delinquents and of eleven of the 500 nondelinquents had not married even after the boys were born.

Another fact of passing interest is that, although there is no difference in the ages of the mothers of the two groups of boys, and practically no difference in the ages of their fathers when the boys were born, their mothers were, on the average, somewhat younger than their fathers. Almost half the mothers of both groups of boys were then under twenty-six.

Six in ten of both the delinquents and the nondelinquents had one or both foreign-born parents. And the parents of both groups had been in America for about the same length of time. This would seem to indicate that these potentials for conflict between the foreign culture of the parents and their American-born sons were similar in the two groups. (It must be remembered that although in this controlled investigation the boys were originally matched on an ethnic-racial basis, this was without regard to whether or not their parents had been born abroad.) Inquiry in the homes of the native-born boys, one or both of whose parents had been born in Europe, resulted in the finding that, despite the fact that culture conflict is frequently cited as a major cause of delinquency and crime, there was actually no greater evidence of clash between the culture of the American-born delinquents and their foreign-born parents than between the American-born nondelinquents and their foreign-born parents, as reflected in such matters as embarrassment or rebellion over the exclusive use of a foreign language in the home, over foreign customs, traditions, disciplinary practices, cookery, and so on. (There are, of course, other sources of culture conflict than those deriving from the foreign background of parents.)

Other vital statistics of interest have to do with the size of the families of which the boys are a part, it being generally supposed that delinquents stem from larger families than do nondelinquents. Although it is recognized that many other variables, such as religious persuasion, economic underprivilege, and immigrant parentage, may account for the size of families, this is less likely to be so in this study in which delinquents and nondelinquents had been matched at the outset in respect to ethnic derivation and residence in under-privileged areas. On the whole, the delinquents did come from only slightly larger families, the average being seven children as compared with six in the households of the nondelinquents. The greater number of children in the homes of the delin-quent boys is partially explainable by the fact that a higher proportion of one or the other of their parents had remarried. Almost a third of the delinquents, as compared with half that proportion of nondelinquents, had half- or stepbrothers and sisters.

Although there was little difference in the size of the house-holds of which the delinquents and the nondelinquents were a part, there was in fact more crowding of living quarters in the homes of the delinquents. It is reasonable to suppose that this resulted in increased competition on the part of the children for parental attention, and in more likelihood of emotional strain, tension, and friction; that it meant loss of privacy, and that therefore it might have induced sexual and other emotional shocks. For example, fewer of the delinquent boys than of the nondelinquents had the exclusive use of a bedroom (two in ten, as compared with three in ten). A high proportion of both groups (over 60 per cent of the delinquents and over 50 per cent of the nondelinquents) had to share a bed with a brother or sister, a parent or another relative, or had to sleep in the same room with more than one brother or sister, or with one or both parents, or with other relatives.

There is one further vital statistic of importance here. This relates to the rank of birth of the boys. Only children, first born children, and youngest children are often thought to be especially vulnerable to the development of behavior diffi-culties, because they are in a pampered position in the family constellation. Contrary to general expectation, how-ever, *lower* proportions of the delinquent boys than of the nondelinquents turned out to be either the only, or first-born, or the youngest arrivals. Although the families are as yet incomplete, the fact that the delinquents and nondelinquents had been matched by age gives this finding significance.

As to the possible extra burden placed upon the parents, especially the mother, by the birth of the boy (as judged by the length of time that had elapsed between his arrival and that of the next older child), there is in fact little difference between the families of the delinquents and of the nondelinquents. They had to meet the problems presented by the birth of a baby after an equal lapse of time following the arrival of the next older child.

Stability of Household

The stability of the home is perhaps the most important single factor to be explored from the point of view of wholesome family life, for here a child's insecurities, his confusions about standards of behavior, and his problem of accepting the authority of parents and others are all involved.

What are the compelling facts?

Clearly the delinquent boys had been subjected to many more unsettling experiences (often, true, because of their own aberrant behavior) than those who were law-abiding. Since uprooting is bound to make excessive demands upon powers of adaptation, it raises or reflects fears and doubts regarding parental understanding, affection, protection, and the relationship to the authoritarian adult world.

A stable household may be described as one in which preferably both parents, but at least one, remain in unbroken physical and affectional relationship to the children except for brief and expectable absences. The measure of household instability was determined by the number of removals of a boy from the particular family group of which he was naturally a part, that is, the home of his parents or, in the event of disruption of the home because of death, desertion, divorce, separation, and the like, the home of the remaining parent, usually the mother. For example, if a boy was removed from the home of his own parents to live in a foster home for more than a brief period (say a few days to a few months) or if he was sent to live with relatives for more than a short time under circumstances representing a break with home ties, this was considered a household change. Temporary departures from home on vacation or brief commitment to a peno-correctional institution or to a hospital for treatment of a physical or mental condition were not looked upon as a breach with the original household.

By the above standards there is no question that the delinquents, as a group, grew up in a far less stable family setting than did the nondelinquents, for a much higher proportion of them than of the nondelinquents (half the former, as contrasted with a tenth of the latter) were exposed to one or more household changes.

In reviewing the life span of the boys, it was found that no fewer than six out of every ten of the homes of the delinquents, as compared with three in ten of the homes of the nondelinquents, had been broken by separation, divorce, death, or the prolonged absence of one of the parents. A little over half these delinquents and only slightly less than half the nondelinquents were still under five years of age when the initial break occurred.

It is probable that the first definitive break in the organic structure of the family is crucial, because it is likely to deal the greatest emotional blow to a child's conception of the solidarity and reliability of the parental team and to disrupt his general sense of security as well as of family stability. In some cases a breach in the family pattern may seriously distort the process of emotional-intellectual identification of a boy with his father as a hero-ideal.

What were the obvious causes of disruption in the family circle, so demoralizing to the growth of a healthy personality?

Here, as in other elements in the under-the-roof situation, the delinquents' families present a much more dismal picture than do those of the law-abiding boys.

Among the delinquents, the first breakup in the family group was, more often than among the nondelinquents, due to the abandonment of the boy at birth or shortly thereafter by parents who had not married each other, or to desertion of the family by one or both parents, or to temporary separation of the parents; or it resulted from prolonged incarceration of a parent. But in the families of the nondelinquent boys the initial breach in the family group was to a greater extent brought about by the death of a parent, or by separation or divorce, or by hospitalization.

In every type of family breach, there was an excess among the homes of the delinquents.

There is no doubt that as the years passed there was a more rapid disintegration of the families of the delinquent boys. Only half the delinquents had the normal experience of being reared continuously by one or both of their own parents, in contrast with nine out of ten of the other boys.[1] These findings, revealing the greater instability of the family life of the boys who got into trouble, reflect again the more extensive and intensive emotional handicaps under which they grew up.

Affectional Ties Between Parents and Boy

But there is one aspect of family life that probably transcends in significance even those already noted, namely, the affectional relationship between the boys and their parents.

[1] This means that, although one parent may have died or left the home, no parent substitute in the person of a stepparent, foster parent, or relative was brought into the family circle.

There is no doubt that a warm tie between father and son is of great significance in helping a boy to develop a wholesome set of ideals through the process of emotional "identification" with his father. Should this bond not be close, the growing child may seek a substitute in companionship with delinquent children; or he may pass through a stage of grave insecurity, frustration, or resentment, with resulting psychoneurotic symptoms. It is highly significant, therefore, that only four out of every ten of the fathers of the delinquents, as compared with eight in ten of the fathers of the nondelinquents, evidenced warmth, sympathy, and affection toward their boys.

So, also, a substantially lower proportion of the mothers of the delinquents (seven in ten, as compared with 95% of the nondelinquents' mothers) held their sons in affectional warmth; but one out of every four of the mothers of the delinquents, in contrast with only one in seven of the latter, showed clear evidence of being overprotective of the boys, an attitude that frequently leads to a crippling childhood dependence which may be carried into adulthood. A far higher proportion of the mothers of the delinquents than of the nondelinquents were openly indifferent or hostile to them, often to the point of rejection.

But parent-child relations are a two-way emotional street. What about the affection of the boys for their parents?

There is widespread acceptance nowadays of the Freudian formulation of the role of close affectional ties between parents and children and the favorable or unfavorable "solution" of that well-known family triangle, the "Oedipus situation," as constituting the very core of personality formation. "It is clear . . . why Freud says that the Oedipus situation is the nuclear complex of all the neuroses. The reaction pattern which the little boy forms to solve these difficult relations with his parents, particularly with his father, serves as the pattern for all his future human relations, whether in the field of love or of business competition. If the solution has been healthy, so will his future human relationships be healthy and be undertaken in the light of their reality. If the solution has been unhealthy he will approach his future relationships with an unhealthy pattern and meet them by this rather than by an intelligent understanding of the real situation."[2] But whether one accepts or rejects the Freudian formula, the emotional attitude of a boy to his parents is a strong indicator of his personality. In the light of this, the findings assume great significance; for a far lower proportion of the delinquents than of the nondelinquents (some three in ten, as contrasted with over six in ten) were found to have close affectional ties to their fathers. And fewer delinquents than nondelinquents had an affectional attachment to their mothers (less than seven in ten as compared with nine in ten). However, a much higher proportion of both groups of boys were held in affectional warmth by their mothers and in turn expressed attachment to their mothers than is true of the situation respecting the fathers.

Experts in dynamic psychiatry are of the opinion that the process of identification of the growing boy with his father, whom he consciously or unconsciously tries to emulate, is highly significant in the development of personality and character. The extent to which the father of a boy was acceptable to him as a figure for identification is revealed in the finding that fewer than two out of ten of the delinquents, as contrasted with over half the nondelinquents considered the father to be the kind of man that he himself would like to be, and had respect for his father's vocational and social standing as well as some sort of common understanding with him.

Information is not available regarding the feelings of the boys toward their brothers and sisters. But some indication of the relation of the boys to them may be inferred from the fact

2 English, O.S., and Pearson, G.H.J., *Common Neuroses of Children and Adults* (New York: W.W. Norton and Company, 1937), p. 44.

that the brothers and sisters were not so warmly attached to the delinquent boys as to the nondelinquents. In some instances, indeed (three in ten among the former as contrasted with less than one in ten among the latter), their brothers and sisters were indifferent or openly hostile to the boy.

Reviewing the data on affectional relations of the family, it must be borne in on us that, all in all, *the delinquent boys were more largely deprived of affection by their fathers, mothers, and brothers and sisters than were the law-abiding youngsters, and that not so many of them as of the nondelinquents responded warmly to their fathers and mothers or developed an emotional tie leading to wholesome identification of boy with father.*

Parental Concern for Boys' Welfare

Psychiatrists and psychologists realize to what extent a child's attitudes and deportment are influenced by his concept, justified or not, of the genuineness of his parents' concern for his well-being. Whatever the outward manifestations of interest may be, it is the feeling of authenticity of the parental attitude, its affectional motivation, and its sincerity that leave a wholesome precipitate in the structure of personality and character. The finding that, as a group, far fewer of the delinquents than of the nondelinquents felt that their mothers and fathers were genuinely concerned about them is of deep significance. Only two in ten of the delinquents, as compared with seven in ten of the nondelinquents, felt that their mothers and fathers were really interested in their welfare.

It is impossible, without deep-probing and time-consuming exploration of the mental life of each boy, to determine how much of this attitude was based upon emotional shocks that he had experienced during the first few years of life, and how much of it is a defense mechanism or a self-deceptive explanation of his behavior. But, in any case, a boy's feeling about his parents' concern for his welfare must play a significant part in determining the path that he will tend to take.

Apart from the feelings of the boys, objective evidence of the lesser concern of the parents for the delinquents is reflected in the vagueness of their plans for the youngsters' future: in more than six out of ten of the cases the delinquents' parents had devoted no thought to this all-important matter, as compared with four in ten of the parents of the nondelinquents.

Further evidence of the lesser concern of the parents of the delinquents for the welfare of the boys derives from the discrepancy between the information given the psychiatrist by the boys themselves about how they use their leisure time and that given by their parents (usually the mothers) to our field investigators. Either the delinquents' parents know far less about how their boys spend their spare hours or for one reason or another preferred not to admit that a boy's habits are bad or that he is running around with questionable companions. By and large, however, it is the impression of the home investigators that the parents of the delinquents were actually unaware of many of the boys' activities.

A reflection of wholesome or unwholesome parent-child relations is furnished by the disciplinary attitudes and practices of mothers and fathers. Such practices are important in guiding children toward a consistent and clear concept of right and wrong and the varying consequences of different types of behavior. But apart from the process of socialization through definition of moral-legal prohibitions, wrong disciplinary practices may have serious consequences in the development of a child's personality, character, and habit systems. Inconsistency between the parents in disciplining a child; excessive anger, unfairness, or other forms of over-emotional response to numerous little peccadilloes normally engaged in by children during the early years when they are testing a developing sense of power may be a baneful source of emotional distortion and ultimately result in ambivalence toward or defiance of the authority of the parents and later of school and society.

The delinquent boys were certainly victims of a far greater laxity on the part of their mothers than were the nondelinquents, for in six in ten instances among the delinquents, as compared with one in ten among the nondelinquents, they paid little attention to the boys' misbehavior. Only a handful of the mothers of the delinquents compared with 60 per cent of the mothers of the nondelinquents met the happy and wholesome mean of both firmness and kindliness in their disciplinary practices. A considerably greater proportion of the mothers of the delinquents than of the nondelinquents were inconsistent in their disciplinary practices, swinging erratically from laxity to overstrictness without apparent reason.

The fathers were generally more inclined than the mothers to be overstrict with the boys. This was characteristic of three out of ten fathers of the delinquents as compared with less than one in ten of the fathers of the nondelinquents. Inconsistent disciplinary practices were also more than twice as prevalent among the fathers of the delinquents.

As regards the methods of discipline, physical punishment seems to have been the favored tool of both the fathers and the mothers of the delinquent boys; for over five of every ten of the mothers and almost seven in ten of the fathers, as compared with three in ten of the mothers and fathers of the nondelinquents, resorted to spankings and whippings in an effort to cope with the misbehavior of the youngsters.

The mothers of both the delinquents and the nondelinquents were considerably more inclined to deprive the boys of privileges rather than to employ the harder measures of punishment resorted to by the fathers.

Fewer of the mothers and fathers of the delinquents than

of the other lads were apt to reason with their sons and try to understand the motives of their misconduct. Relatively few of the parents in both groups made any attempt to appeal to a boy's self-respect, conscience, social ideals, or family name.

All in all, the most marked difference between the disciplinary practices of the parents of the delinquents and those of the nondelinquents is found in the considerably greater resort of the former to physical punishment and the lesser extent to which they calmly reasoned with the boys about their misconduct. It may well be that the delinquent boys, being so continually involved in misbehavior, called forth more rigid or more erratic controls on the part of their parents. But whether this be so or not, the above analysis is, among other things, a revealing commentary on the relative ineffectiveness of physical punishment in managing a boy's misconduct.

In this chapter we have seen that, as to certain situational factors involved in the foundations of parent-child relations, the delinquents and nondelinquents resembled each other—in age of their parents at the birth of the boys, in certain potentials for culture conflict, and in the frequency of the advent of children in the family.

The delinquents stemmed from only slightly larger families than did the nondelinquents. In the family constellation, fewer of them were among those generally deemed more vulnerable to emotional trauma in their intrafamily relations, that is, only children, first-born, or youngest children.

With reference to the more dynamic arena of parent-child relations, the delinquents, as a group, were excessively the victims not only of unstable households but of out-and-out broken homes. To a far greater extent than the nondelinquents they had substitute parents (foster or stepparents) or lived with relatives.

As regards affectional relations between the parents and the boys, so crucial to the development of personality and character, many more of the delinquents were the victims of the indifference or actual hostility of their fathers and mothers; and they, in turn, were less attached to their parents. Not only did they draw less affection from their mothers and fathers, but they were also treated with less warmth by their brothers and sisters. This greater emotional deprivation is further reflected in a more frequently expressed feeling on the part of the delinquent boys that their parents were not concerned about their welfare. Whether as a result of this or of other elements in the family life, not nearly so many delinquents as nondelinquents identified themselves with, or sought to emulate, their fathers.

How much this, in turn, was cause or consequence of the more erratic discipline imposed on the delinquent boys by their fathers and the fathers' far greater resort to physical punishment can only be surmised. The mothers of the delinquents, though not so inconsistent in their disciplinary practices, were, however, far more lax than the fathers. Fewer of both the mothers and the fathers of the delinquents than of the law-abiding lads were firm and kindly in their disciplinary practices.

There is, therefore, abundant evidence for the conclusion that *the lawbreakers, far more than the nondelinquents, grew up in a family atmosphere not conducive to the development of emotionally well-integrated, happy youngsters, conditioned to obey legitimate authority.*

CHAPTER VII

The Boy in School

Under the impact of intensive clinical exploration of human motives and behavior, it is being realized more and more that "book learning" does not play as important a role in the development of character and conduct as was formerly supposed. Knowledge is one thing; its efficient and socially acceptable use is quite another. The child's instinctual drives, his emotional moods and impulses, and his temperamental equipment are inevitably involved in the proper use of the instruments he obtains through the gateway of learning.

Nevertheless, it is important to find out as much as possible about the school experiences of our two groups of boys; for, though schooling does not completely account for the structuring of character and the motivation of conduct, it can provide a sense of emotional satisfaction in the achievement of skills; it can arouse socially acceptable ambitions; it can place the pupil in contact with adults with whom he can identify and whom he can strive to emulate. On the other hand, it can leave scars in the psyche of the growing child which may well enhance the development of antisocial attitudes and defiance of all authority.

The school is the child's first testing ground outside the secure atmosphere of his home. It supplies the first proof of his adaptability and his capacity for socialization in a theater of action in which there are strict rules punitively enforced by nonparental authority. In school the child gets his first taste of the power of the outside world to impose rigid standards of behavior and to subject the individual to restraints and punishments from which even loving and protective parents are often unable to save him. Outside the familiar home atmosphere the child is forced to face reality and to prove his capacity to sink or swim.

School Status

Although the delinquents and the nondelinquents had originally been matched by age and intelligence, we found when we first encountered them that twice as many of the delinquents had not yet gone beyond the sixth grade and that an excessive proportion of the former were still below the sixth grade level or had been placed in special classes. At the advanced end of the scale, only half as many delinquents as nondelinquents had reached junior high or high school. As a group, the delinquents were a year behind the nondelinquents in educational achievement, the average grade attained by the former being the seventh, and by the latter the eighth.

Of course, the delinquents may have had to repeat grades now and then because of commitment to correctional schools and placement in foster homes as a result of their antisocial behavior, but this only partially accounts for the difference in grade attained.

Although both delinquents and nondelinquents entered school at the same age, the delinquents were shifted about more from one school to another, not only as a result of occasional placement in foster homes (usually in rural districts) by the correctional authorities but because their families moved about more frequently than did the families of the nondelinquents, and also because more of their homes were disrupted. About four in ten of the delinquents had been pupils in more than five different schools, as compared with two in ten of the nondelinquents. On the average, the delinquents attended nearly six schools, the nondelinquents four and a half. This more frequent shifting from school to school partly explains why a far higher proportion of the delinquents repeated two or more school grades; other reasons are noted below.

School Retardation

Regarding backwardness in school, twice as many delinquents as nondelinquents were two or more years behind the proper grade for their age. Considering only those boys who were markedly retarded (three years or more), there is an even more striking difference between the delinquents and the nondelinquents, amounting to thrice the proportion of excessive retardation among the former as among the latter (23%:8%). Their marked backwardness is further reflected by the fact that twice as many of the delinquents (two in ten as compared with one in ten) had been in special classes for retarded children at one time or another. Although some of this retardation may be accounted for by less regular attendance (brought about by delinquency), it certainly cannot all be charged to this; for there was an educational program in the correctional schools to fill the gaps that occurred by the interruption of the regular schooling of the delinquents.

These differences assume added significance in the light of the initial matching of the delinquents and nondelinquents in general intelligence level.

Some of the reasons for the greater school retardation of the delinquents have been derived from interviews with their most recent teachers. According to them, half the delinquent group manifested a lack of interest in schoolwork, as compared with fewer than two in ten of the nondelinquents; half the former and a fifth of the latter were "inattentive;" almost half the delinquents as compared with one in five of the nondelinquents were described as "careless;" two in five contrasted with one in five of the nondelinquents were reported to be "lazy." Their most recent teachers reported that a fifth of the delinquents and a tenth of the nondelinquents were frequently tardy, and in similar proportions they were described as "restless."

Subject Preferences

Turning now to preferences for certain subjects and marked dislike for others, the psychiatrist (Dr. Bryant E. Moulton, formerly of the Judge Baker Guidance Centre of Boston) sought to determine from the boys what school studies they especially liked, recording only those for which a boy could give definite reasons.

The delinquents as well as the nondelinquents who expressed strong preferences said they liked courses in the manual arts best (63%:59%). They did not differ appreciably in the other subjects for which they expressed real interest. Both groups of boys showed little enthusiasm for arithmetic, social studies, art courses, English (including reading and spelling), science courses, commercial subjects, foreign languages. Perhaps this is characteristic of boys of limited cultural background reared in the submerged areas of our larger cities.

Similar proportions of delinquents and nondelinquents expressed strong dislikes for English, reading, and spelling (42%:40%); but more of the former than of the latter had no liking for arithmetic (54%:43%); social studies (21%: 12%); foreign languages (19%:5%); the arts (14%:6%); science courses (14%:4%); and commercial subjects (11%: 2%).

The above brief analysis of marked subject likes and dislikes indicates, on the whole, not too striking a variance in the intellectual tastes of the two groups. In quite similar and considerable proportions, the delinquents and the nondelinquents were "hand-minded," strongly preferring manual training and particularly disliking such intellectual and verbal disciplines as English, reading, and spelling. However, there was even greater distaste among the delinquents not only for subjects requiring strict logical reasoning and persistency of effort (arithmetic, science) but also for those calling for good memory (e.g., foreign languages).

Scholarship and Achievement

Judging the differences in scholarship and achievement of both groups of boys by their actual accomplishment during their last full year of school, it was possible to ascertain from the school records that four in ten of the delinquent boys, compared with but one in ten of the nondelinquents, were poor students, as reflected by marks of D and E in most or all subjects. While nine out of every ten of the nondelinquents were average pupils (the B and C group), less than six in ten of the delinquents attained such status. A mere handful (1%) of each group of boys excelled in their studies, as indicated by an almost all-A record.

There can be no question, therefore, that, despite their essential similarity in age and intelligence quotient, and taking into account the greater irregularity in the school attendance, the educational attainments of the delinquents were far below those of the nondelinquents.

Confirmation of this is derived from the differences in their status in reading and arithmetic, as ascertained through Stanford Achievement Tests.[1] In comparing the average reading quotients of delinquents and nondelinquents, we found a

[1] While it is impossible to say that any tests can distinguish sharply between inherited and acquired abilities, achievement tests are designed to elicit the degree of learning actually reached following a period of instruction. We do not overlook the fact that inadequacies in achievement involve, on the one hand, innate deficiencies and, on the other, many extraneous factors such as emotional distress, poor habits of study, truancy, dislike of school, and the like.

five-point difference in favor of the nondelinquents. Although not large, this is statistically significant. For example, many more delinquents than nondelinquents (54%:36%) had a reading quotient of less than 80 points. In arithmetic also the delinquents achieved less, as reflected in an average for the group of 71 as compared with 78 attained by the nondelinquents.

There was a greater scattering or variability among the delinquents on the subtests of the reading and arithmetic scales.

Attitude Toward School

Slower progress through the grades, poorer scholarship, fewer preferences and more marked dislikes for certain school subjects, as well as greater erraticism (scatter or variability) in their performance, all point toward greater antipathy of the delinquents for school. This is borne out not only by their teachers, who found the delinquents to be far less interested in school, but also by the revelations made by the boys to the psychiatrist. Many a delinquent would spontaneously state, "I hate school because I am always left back," or "It is too hard," or "I want to go to work," and so on. Only one in ten of the delinquents readily accepted schooling, as compared with almost seven in ten of the nondelinquents.

The reasons the delinquents gave for their marked dislike of school, apart from intellectual inferiority, are largely reflective of temperamental and emotional difficulties—inability to learn, lack of interest, resentment of restriction and routine.

The greater dislike for school on the part of the delinquents is further revealed by the nature of their academic and vocational ambitions. Although some of both delinquents and nondelinquents had not as yet given any thought to whether they wished to stop school or continue into high school, a far higher proportion of all the delinquents (four in ten as compared with one in ten of the nondelinquents) wanted to stop school immediately. Contrariwise, a much lower proportion (three in ten: seven in ten) wanted to go on to high or trade school; while only fourteen delinquents, as compared with fifty-seven nondelinquents, expressed any desire for education beyond high school.

When they were questioned about the kind of pursuits in which they would like to engage after completing their schooling, three out of ten of the delinquents as compared with two in ten of the nondelinquents expressed vague, childish, superficial, or unrealistic notions about this. However, among the delinquents as a group there was more of an inclination to adventurous occupations, such as aviation, going to sea, joining the Armed Services (two in ten as compared with one in ten); and a few expressed a preference for jobs not requiring much training. As might be anticipated, a lower proportion of the delinquents than of the nondelinquents wished to learn a trade or wanted to engage in intellectual pursuits or in aesthetic or artistic callings.

From the nature of their academic and vocational ambitions, it is clear that the delinquent group as a whole had less desire than the nondelinquents either for formal schooling or for vocational training, and that they had, in fact, given less thought to planning their future.

Relation to Schoolmates

Recent teachers of the boys were questioned in regard to the boys' relationship to their fellow pupils. If a boy got on well with other children, was friendly, and made an effort to please and hold friends, his relationship to them was categorized as *good*. A considerably lower proportion of the delinquents than of the nondelinquents (four and a half in ten as compared with seven in ten) could be so classified.

If a boy, though not seeking the companionship of other

children in school, was not actively antagonistic to any of them, his relationship to his schoolmates was described as *fair*. This was found to be the case among about a third of the delinquents compared to a fourth of the nondelinquents.

If, however, a boy was pugnacious or unfriendly and other children did not like him, his relationship to his schoolmates was considered *poor*. In this category fell a considerably higher proportion of the delinquents than of the nondelinquents (two in ten as compared with less than one in ten).

Earliest School Misbehavior

Before tracing the school misbehavior of the boys to its beginnings, we must record the striking fact that *no less than nine in ten of the delinquents persistently (and often seriously) misconducted themselves in school*[2] *at one time or another compared to less than two in ten of the nondelinquents.*

That the tendency to maladapted and antisocial behavior is early and deeply rooted among the delinquents is already evident. Careful reconstruction of their school careers has revealed that almost a third of the delinquents who misbehaved in school were under eight years old when the first signs of maladapted behavior occurred in school. The delinquents as a whole were much younger than the relatively few nondelinquents whose misconduct was so serious or persistent as to be forced upon the teacher's attention, the average age of 478 delinquents at their first school misbehavior being nine and a half and of 86 nondelinquents, twelve and a half.

Further reflecting the deep-rootedness of the tendency to maladaptation among the delinquents is the fact of their being in lower grades when their school misconduct first became evident. As many as 18% of the 478 delinquents who

2 This encompasses truancy, stealing, persistent attempts to attract attention, inattention, mischievousness, disobedience, defiance, stubbornness, carelessness, lying, underhandedness, sexual misconduct, smoking.

markedly misbehaved were in kindergarten or first grade at the time, as compared with 6% of the 86 misbehaving nondelinquents. Three-fourths of the very large group of delinquents who misconducted themselves in school were in grades lower than the sixth at the time, as compared with a fourth of the few misbehaving nondelinquents.

It would appear, therefore, that *difficulties in social adaptation as manifested by school misconduct were clearly evident among the delinquents prior to the onset of puberty, while in the case of the few nondelinquents who had behavioral difficulties in school, these did not show themselves until puberty and early adolescence.*

The vast majority (95%) of the delinquents had truanted at one time or another during their school careers, while only one in ten of the nondelinquents had ever truanted, and then only occasionally. Of the 474 delinquents who were school truants, two-thirds frequently "skipped school."

It is clear, therefore, that social maladjustment expressed itself throughout the school careers of the delinquent boys, not only by disobedience, unruliness, defiance, stubbornness, or temper tantrums and the like, but by running away from difficult or unpleasant social situations and obligations, and often, as we shall see later, toward more absorbing activities.

Almost half the delinquents who truanted from school began to do so before they were ten years old, while of the handful of nondelinquents who truanted occasionally most were eleven or older when they first skipped school. The average age at which the delinquents began to truant was ten, that of the nondelinquents twelve and a half.

In order that we might determine how the delinquents and the nondelinquents behaved in school during their most recent full school year, the latest teacher of each boy was provided with a list of behavior characteristics and asked to check them. Although the results can hardly be looked upon as complete or definitive because of some variation in the interpretation of certain of the behavior characteristics by so many teachers in so many different schools, the general trend of differences between the two groups is unmistakable.[3]

With the exception of a few behavior traits in which the incidence among delinquents and nondelinquents was similar ("dreaminess," nervousness, thoughtlessness, sensitiveness, fearfulness) or in which the *nondelinquents* exceeded the delinquents (whispering and shyness), the delinquents came far more sharply to the attention of their teachers by their troublesome behavior. In order of incidence, a much higher proportion of the delinquents than of the nondelinquents showed lack of interest in their schoolwork; were unreliable, inattentive, careless, lazy, untruthful; were disobedient, tardy, attention seeking, and disorderly in class. Almost a fifth of the delinquent group compared to not one of the nondelinquents stole in school. Their teachers also reported that more of the delinquents than of the other boys cheated or smoked in school; more were easily discouraged, stubborn, unhappy, restless, suggestible, depressed. More of the delinquents than of the control group were characterized by their teachers as defiant, resentful, sullen, unsocial, impudent. More wrote obscene notes or talked obscenely. More were quarrelsome, domineering, cruel, bullying; more showed themselves to be physical cowards; more were selfish, suspicious; more resorted to lying and profanity; more destroyed school materials.

The foregoing description of the outstanding school differences between the boys who got into persistent trouble with the law and those who remained law-abiding shows that very early in life there were clear signals of rough seas ahead.

[3] The reader is asked to bear in mind that, although most of the delinquents had not been under the observation of their teachers for some months, i.e., since their most recent commitment to a correctional school, the nondelinquents were currently known to their teachers.

Despite the original matching of the boys by age and general intelligence, and despite the similarity of the two groups in the age at which they entered the first grade, the delinquents were definitely more retarded scholastically than the nondelinquents. The greater moving about to which the delinquents were subjected, their more frequent placement in foster homes following the disruption of their own homes, their commitment to correctional institutions—these facts do not completely account for the excessive repetition of grades and marked backwardness in terms of achievement as it relates to age and grade placement.

Although the delinquents and the nondelinquents, in like proportions, preferred manual training and disliked verbal disciplines, there was a more prevalent distaste among the delinquents not only for subjects requiring strict logical reasoning and persistency of effort but also for those dependent upon good memory.

To a much greater extent than the nondelinquents, the law violators expressed violent dislike of school, resentment at its restrictions, and lack of interest in school work. On the other hand, the few nondelinquents who found school distasteful said it was largely because they were unable to learn and because they felt intellectually inferior.

The school attainment of the delinquents was far below that of the nondelinquents. The delinquents were also somewhat more variable or erratic in their school accomplishment as reflected by Achievement Tests in reading and arithmetic.

As to their academic ambitions, a markedly higher proportion of the delinquents expressed a desire to stop school at once, while many more nondelinquents planned to go on to high school, trade school, or beyond.

In vocational ambitions, likewise, the delinquents differed from the nondelinquents, a higher proportion of the former expressing childish notions about what they wanted to do in life or inclining to adventurous occupations and to work requiring little training, instead of to trades and intellectual pursuits.

In their interpersonal relationships with schoolmates, the delinquents were less friendly and more pugnacious.

Marked differences between the two groups also were noted in respect to conduct in school. More than nine-tenths of the delinquents seriously or persistently misbehaved in school as compared with less than two in ten of the nondelinquents, their misconduct running the entire gamut of school offenses. Truancy was the most uniform manifestation of maladjustment among the 478 delinquents who misbehaved in school. The various indications of maladaptation and misconduct in school occurred at a much earlier age among the delinquents than among the small group of 86 nondelinquents whose conduct was poor in school. This is clearly indicative of the relative *deep-rootedness of the emotional difficulties and antisocial habits of the delinquents.*

It is evident that the traits and tendencies in the form of social maladaptation which the law, representing society in general, calls "delinquency" are also expressed in excessive maladaptation to the code of behavior governing the smaller society, the school. When, therefore, the law at last takes hold, the antisocial attitudes and habits, and the personality and character distortions, are far deeper than the delinquent act itself would indicate. Much damage has already been done inside as well as outside the delinquent boy.

How to detect early enough the danger signals of persistent maladapted behavior in order to cope with it before it becomes habitual is a crucial problem we must face.

CHAPTER VIII

The Boy on the Streets

We have seen that the homes of the delinquent boys were far less adequate than those of the law-abiders, not only in physical attributes but in the quality of the family life. We can therefore conclude that the delinquents had less reason than the nondelinquents to be attached to their homes.

Thus handicapped, they were also exposed to worse influences in the streets, in jobs, in recreations, and in companionships than were the nondelinquents. True, they all—delinquents as well as nondelinquents—lived in unwholesome neighborhoods. If we examine their street activities, we may learn how and why a similar cultural matrix has somehow squeezed some boys into different shapes of delinquency while permitting others to remain nondelinquents.

Neighborhood Ties

Selected from badly deteriorated or rapidly deteriorating areas of a large city, a great proportion of both delinquents and nondelinquents were found to have lived in such neighborhoods all their lives. If they were removed from such regions it was only for brief periods: in the case of 88 delinquents, because of placement in foster homes by courts, parole officers, social agencies, and occasionally by their own families, in an effort to counteract deleterious home and street influences; and in the case of 17 nondelinquents, generally because of their placement by welfare agencies necessitated by illness of the parents or disruption of the home. Only five delinquents and twelve nondelinquents had lived in rural communities or small towns throughout their lives except for the last few years.

Frequent moving about means relative anonymity and the likelihood of failure to develop a feeling of loyalty and responsibility to neighbors; it tends rather to develop a sense of instability. In the past, life was lived in one small community, and everyone was known to his neighbors, a fact which made for relative unity of cultural values and exerted a certain disciplinary influence on conduct.

To what extent did the boys have the opportunity to take root in a neighborhood?

As might be expected, we found that the delinquents had far less chance than the other boys to develop neighborhood ties, for four-fifths had moved five times or more as compared with two-fifths of the nondelinquents. One out of every three of the delinquents had changed residence eleven or more times, as compared with but one in ten of the nondelinquents. Although a fourth of each group had moved five, six, or seven times—which, in view of the fact that the boys averaged fourteen and a half years when selected for the research, means less often than once a year—more than half the delinquents had been uprooted eight or more times.

Thus, whatever the effect of greater mobility upon a tendency to disregard neighborhood opinion as a guide to behavior, it must have operated much more excessively upon the delinquents than upon the nondelinquents.

The delinquent boys were also more markedly subjected to unusual environmental experiences. Taking into account excessive running away from home or bunking out, placement in foster homes (including homes of relatives), removal to orphanages and similar protective institutions, placement in

schools for the feeble-minded, and commitment to correctional schools (excluding, however, the most recent commitment), and time spent in foreign countries, a much higher
proportion of the delinquents than of the nondelinquents
(seven in ten as compared with one in ten) underwent such
unsettling environmental experiences. These undoubtedly
demanded frequent readaptations to situations, companions,
and activities.

A third of 357 delinquents were removed from or left the
family home for reasons having to do with their antisocial
behavior, which resulted either in placement in a correctional
school, or in court order for placement in a foster home or in
a nonpenal institution. Almost another third ran away from
home or bunked out. However, a considerably *lower* proportion of the delinquent group than of the 47 nondelinquents
who left the parental roof had to do so because of the breakup
of the household resulting from death, desertion, separation,
or divorce of the parents; or because of the parents' financial
inability to care for the boy.

All in all, among some two-thirds of 357 delinquents, as contrasted with not one of the 47 nondelinquents who separated
from their families, the reasons for the first departure from
home can be charged to the boy's own misconduct (delinquency, running away, bunking out); while in contrast, all
the nondelinquents compared to a third of the delinquents
had left the parental roof as a result of situations beyond their
control (disruption of the home, parents' financial inability
to care for the boy, unsuitability of the home, illness of the
parents, or illness of the boy himself).

Employment After School

Working after school hours can have either desirable consequences in teaching elementary business practices and
contributing to a sense of economic responsibility or harmful

ones in developing a premature sophistication and subjecting a boy too early to the hazards of life in the city streets.

How do the delinquents and the nondelinquents compare in this respect?

The great majority of both groups (84% of the delinquents, 78% of the nondelinquents) worked after school for varying periods of time, most of them deriving their spending money entirely from their earnings.

Nearly half the delinquents and nondelinquents who were thus employed worked daily; one in four were employed only during weekends or vacations. Somewhat more of the delinquents than the other boys worked regularly.

Very little difference was found in the reasons for after-school work of the two groups of boys. Quite similar proportions took jobs because they wanted to have spending money, or because they were urged to do so by their families, or enjoyed the prestige of being wage earners, or wanted to help their families.

Although delinquents and nondelinquents worked after school hours with about equal regularity and for similar reasons, more than half the former, as compared with a third of the latter, gravitated principally to street trades, such as peddling, bootblacking, and selling newspapers, which means that they were more exposed to street influences than the nondelinquents. Correlatively, a considerably lower proportion of the delinquents (8%:25%) were mainly engaged in jobs in which some supervision and protection was provided—as office boys or store helpers. In equal proportion the two groups took work as delivery boys, errand boys, or messengers, or any odd jobs they could pick up. Few of either group found work in factories.

Thus, the delinquents on the whole sought out the more hazardous and adventuresome jobs in which they were less subject to protection from vicious street influences.

Use of Leisure

There are many indications that, despite their working after school, the boys had a considerable amount of leisure time. Only one in five of the delinquent boys and a little over two-fifths of the nondelinquents were assigned any regular household tasks to keep them occupied, such as running errands, making their own beds, setting the table, helping with the dishes, emptying garbage and ashes, bringing up coal, and the like. A third of the delinquents and a fifth of the nondelinquents were occasionally asked to run errands or do some repair work or help with a furnace, but they were not tied to any specific hours in carrying out their sporadic duties. Almost half the delinquents and a third of the nondelinquents were not required by their families to assist in the household in any way. Here is further evidence of unwise parental supervision in missing the opportunity to give the boys practice in assuming part of the obligation of family living.

How, then, did the boys use their spare time?

Information as to the manner in which delinquents and nondelinquents spent their leisure hours was collated from several sources—interviews with the boys, interviews with their parents (usually their mothers), and sometimes with older brothers and sisters; interviews with the boys' most recent teachers; records of welfare agencies, settlement houses, boys' clubs, and other recreational centers.

The boys were encouraged to give spontaneous expression to their recreational preferences, such as playing football, going to the movies, riding a bicycle, playing with a gang, and so on. Their activities were classified into the following types: *adventurous* (amusements involving excitement, risk, daring, such as "hopping trucks"); *competitive* (sports or games in which there is rivalry between individuals or teams, such as baseball, football, basketball); *active noncompetitive* (amusements that involve much bodily action but in which the element of competition is usually absent, such as hiking, swimming, bicycling); *nonactive* (quiet amusements lacking in action or competition, such as being a spectator at events, movies, reading, indoor hobbies).

A much higher proportion of the delinquents than of the nondelinquents expressed a preference for *adventurous activities* (48%:10%). A lower percentage preferred active sports free of the element of competition (37%:47%). Far fewer delinquents than nondelinquents (8%:29%) chose competitive sports or games, and fewer were content with quiet amusements.

This definite preference of the delinquents as a group for adventurous, exciting forms of recreation is striking. It is probably related to findings from other lines of the inquiry separately pursued; for example, to the greater restlessness of the delinquents. It is a fact that the mothers of the boys reported to the interviewers that over half the delinquents, compared with less than a third of the nondelinquents, had been extremely restless from their earliest years.

A greater thirst for excitement on the part of the delinquents was also disclosed in far more frequent movie attendance. Almost half of them, compared with a tenth of the law-abiding boys, attended movies excessively (three or more times weekly); while almost half the nondelinquents, compared with one in seven of the delinquents, were content (or were permitted) to attend the movies no more than once a week. It would seem that the vicarious excitement of motion-picture thrillers is a way of satisfying the strong craving for adventure which characterizes delinquents. Not only in real life, therefore, but also in make-believe, the troublesome boy has a more powerful urge than the nondelinquent for exciting outlets.

Adventurous Activities

But the reality of this greater thirst for excitement among the delinquents is brought home still more strikingly in their other activities. Over nine-tenths of them, as compared with less than a fourth of the nondelinquents, were in the habit of stealing rides or hopping trucks; over nine-tenths, compared with less than a tenth of the others, kept late hours, roaming about the streets after dark; 90% and 23%, respectively, began to smoke at an early age; 29%, compared with 0.4%, began to drink before or during their early teens; 67%, as contrasted with 10%, made a practice of sneaking into movies; and 62% and 4%, respectively, indulged in various acts of destructive mischief. To this striking evidence must be added the finding that 59% of the delinquents, in contrast with but 1% of the non-offenders, ran away from home; that 59%, compared with 2%, "bunked out;" that 53% and 9%, respectively, gambled (largely "shooting craps"); and that 13% and 0.4%, respectively, set fires.

Could there be a much more convincing demonstration that *in all the major forms of exciting youthful activity afforded by the deteriorated American urban area, the delinquents as a group greatly exceeded the boys who remained law-abiding?*

But here is further evidence.

Almost all the delinquents (95%), as compared with three-fifths of the nondelinquents, were in the habit of hanging around street corners; 87% of them compared to 14% of the nondelinquents sought their recreations in regions considerably distant from their own homes; many more delinquents than nondelinquents played in vacant lots (46%:27%), on the waterfronts (30%:16%), and in railroad yards (20%: 1%); many more frequented poolrooms, dance halls, penny arcades, and similar places of commercialized recreation (15%:0.8%).

By contrast, a much *lower* proportion of the delinquents than of the law-abiding youngsters spent at least some of their leisure hours at home (42%:93%), or on playgrounds (29%:61%).

Possibly the fact that the delinquents were more risk-taking and roamed about much more than the nondelinquents explains the finding that a considerably higher proportion of them met with serious accidents, most of which took place in the streets. Fully 14 per cent of the delinquents, as compared with five per cent of the nondelinquents, were struck down by moving vehicles—automobiles, trucks, motorcycles, bicycles, and the like. Again 19% of the delinquents, compared with 10% of the nondelinquents, suffered from other kinds of serious accidents, most of them the result of falling from moving vehicles or from high places—roofs, windows, fences, bridges, lampposts.

Companions

Much has been written and spoken about bad companions and membership in gangs as causes of delinquency; and it has been taken for granted that, living in slum areas, most boys would be "infected" by the bad companion who plays the role of the proverbial rotten apple in the barrel. But boys are not apples. They tend to be attracted to, or to choose companions who are congenial to them. Thus, over half the boys who were delinquents became members of gangs, while only three of the lads who remained nondelinquent joined gangs. The troublesome lads seem far less content than the nondelinquents with a few friends or even with a "crowd," as opposed to a formalized gang. *However, by and large, they were maladjusted and delinquent children long before they were gang members.* Gang membership may have multiplied their antisocial activities; it rarely originated persistent delinquency.

The delinquents almost without exception chummed largely with other delinquents, while the nondelinquents, despite the fact that they too lived in the slums, had few intimates among delinquents. This does not mean that they were not rubbing shoulders with them; it does mean that they did not choose delinquents as bosom friends. Thus the evidence would strongly suggest that the tendency to develop companionships selectively is a much more fundamental fact in any analysis of the causes of juvenile crime than the psychologically naïve theory that "differential association" of nondelinquent boys with delinquents is the basic cause of delinquency.

Almost half the delinquents were attracted to youths older than themselves, compared with only one in ten of the nondelinquents; fewer of the former were inclined to choose companions of their own age or younger than themselves. This greater tendency of the delinquents to seek companions among older youths may be associated with the search for a substitute "ego-ideal" to look up to, admire, and emulate; for as we have seen, their fathers were less sympathetic and less acceptable as admired models than were the fathers of the nondelinquents.

Although the majority of both groups of boys were not as yet particularly "girl-minded," nevertheless a higher proportion of the delinquents sought the companionship of girls. Bearing in mind that the delinquents and nondelinquents were matched by age, the greater interest of the former in companions of the opposite sex may be reflective of their greater sexual precocity, although it may also indicate less supervision by their parents. The probability of greater sexual precocity is supported by the finding that at least 19% of the delinquents (compared with 2% of the nondelinquents) had already had heterosexual experiences; that 21% of the delinquents (and 1% of the nondelinquents) had indulged in various forms of sex play; and that 29% of the delinquents (and 3% of the nondelinquents) were excessive masturbators.

Supervised Recreations

We have seen that the delinquents employed their free hours more dangerously than the other boys. What part did the community's agencies for the wholesome and constructive use of leisure play in their lives?

In view of the high degree of organization of club activities for boys in the Boston area in recent years, it is not surprising to find that nine out of every ten of *both* the delinquents and the nondelinquents had at one time or another some contact with boys' clubs, settlement houses, or similar supervised recreational services.

It does not follow, however, that their participation in such activities was necessarily more than casual. The fact is that of the 343 delinquents and 334 nondelinquents from whom information was elicited concerning the regularity of their use of organized recreational facilities, 60% of the delinquents attended clubs twice or more a week, as compared with 73% of the nondelinquents; while a far greater proportion of the delinquents (25% as compared with 10%) attended on extraordinary occasions only, such as the showing of a movie, an athletic contest, or some other event in which they had some special interest.

Furthermore, of the 229 delinquents and 230 nondelinquents from whom it was possible to determine reasons for attending boys' clubs, it transpired that a fourth of the delinquents did so upon the insistence of their parole or probation officers. A third more were urged to do so by their parents or other authoritative adults, this being also true of a third of the nondelinquents. A considerably lower proportion of the delinquents than of the nondelinquents (26%:48%) joined clubs as a result of urging from companions; equally small numbers of the delinquents and nondelinquents attended clubs because of pressure from brothers and sisters; while a few of both the delinquents and the nondelinquents, but more of the latter, joined purely of their own volition.

Viewing the situation as a whole, it would appear that more than half the delinquents were directed to organized recreational activities by adults in authority over them (probation and parole officers, parents, teachers, and so on), and that seven in ten of the nondelinquents participated of their own volition or upon the suggestion of playmates or brothers and sisters.

The fact that the delinquents needed more urging to take part in club programs, attend settlement houses and similar recreational centers, would seem to reflect a lesser desire among them for *organized* and *supervised* activities.

It was possible to gain from 310 delinquents and 293 nondelinquents some idea of their attitude toward supervised recreation. Twice as many delinquents as nondelinquents (21%:12%) expressed a marked dislike or contempt for the controlled recreations provided in clubs, playgrounds, or school gymnasiums. On the other hand, more nondelinquents than delinquents (38%:18%) were enthusiastic about supervised activities, expressing real preference for them, and also indicating that to some extent they welcomed protection against overly rough or inconsiderate competition. But over half of both delinquents and nondelinquents were vague in their attitude toward supervised recreation, either because they had not given any thought to the matter or were really indifferent; or they indicated that their like or dislike of group activities depended on whether or not their friends participated in them. Because of the small numbers of those who made their feelings sufficiently clear, these findings must be treated with caution. Nevertheless, the difference between the delinquents and the nondelinquents in inclination toward supervised recreation is suggestive and in harmony with other findings in the study. Intensive research into the recreational interests of different types of boys, especially delinquents, is obviously needed. In the guidance of boys into wholesome channels for outlet of energy, it is too often a case of "you can bring a horse to the water (or bring the water to the horse) but you cannot make him drink without he will."

Needed, also, is investigation into forms of recreation that will attract family groups as a whole instead of enhancing the tendency to divisiveness in family life.

Church Attendance

How did the boys compare in attention to their religious duties? The delinquents as a group were found to be less conscientious about their religious obligations than the nondelinquents, about four in ten of them as compared to almost seven in ten of the nondelinquents attending church once a week. However, only a small proportion of either group neglected their religious duties completely. As in the case of recreational activities, so in church attendance, no intensive exploration was made of the reasons for the lesser adherence of the delinquents to their religious duties.

We have seen that, although the two sets of boys had been matched on the basis of residence in underprivileged urban environments, there were certain inevitable differences in their early experiences attributable to the fact that the families of the delinquents moved more frequently and that the delinquents experienced more frequent changes of environment stemming in part at least from their antisocial behavior.

Granting these differences, it must be apparent from the array of findings that antisocial behavior cannot be ascribed largely to the influences of the slums. Human motivation and human conduct are not so simple. The impact of the sociocultural matrix on the two sets of boys was found to have varied considerably. And this was to be expected. For human beings are not entirely robots passively influenced in like manner and degree by environmental-cultural stimuli. They express some selective powers in absorbing and rejecting bits or patterns of a complex environmental pressure system.

For example, a considerably higher proportion of the delinquents than of the control group preferred to work in street trades, while more of the latter selected jobs in which some supervision was provided. As a group, the delinquents were definitely more inclined to adventurous activities. This tendency was found to be reflected in the greater proportion of them who went to the movies frequently, who hopped trucks, stole rides, kept late hours, smoked and drank at an early age, sneaked into theaters without paying, committed destructive mischief, ran away from home and school, bunked out, gambled, begged on the streets, set fires, and the like.

Further evidence of their excessive craving for excitement and adventure was found in the far greater proportion of delinquents who hung about street corners; sought their recreations in neighborhoods distant from their homes; played in vacant lots, on waterfronts, and in railroad yards; frequented cheap poolrooms, dance halls, and the like. By contrast, many more nondelinquents found at least some of their recreations at home or on playgrounds.

Regarding the companionships of the two groups of boys, the delinquents gravitated to gangs, while the nondelinquents avoided them almost entirely, preferring a few intimates, largely nondelinquents like themselves. The delinquents, however, not only chummed largely with other delinquents but attached themselves to older boys.

While almost all the boys had contact with boys' clubs, settlement houses, and other agencies of supervised recreation, far less initiative in seeking such outlets was shown by the delinquents, and they attended clubs less frequently and spontaneously. Almost twice as many delinquents as other boys expressed a marked dislike for organized and supervised recreations.

Finally, the delinquents attended church with far less regularity than did the nondelinquents; albeit only a small proportion of either group neglected their religious duties entirely.

When these facts are reflected upon, it becomes clear that in order to understand the impact of the milieu on those who live and act therein, findings regarding the varying rates of delinquency in different zones or areas of a city are of dim and superficial illumination. For, given a similar general deteriorated and economically disadvantaged environment, the response of different individuals to some of its elements may be uniform, but to others it is unquestionably varied and selective.

In this chapter we have derived some hints of the possible reasons for this selectivity of response to the general culture of a region. Other hints may come from other parts of the inquiry. In the meantime it is clear that in addition to the marked disadvantages already shown to exist among the delinquents in respect to their parental and home backgrounds, the influences of the streets have selectively played their unwholesome role.

CHAPTER IX

Physique and Delinquency

In the preceding chapters we have described the various theaters of action in which our boys spent their formative years. We now turn to the characteristics of the boys themselves, because how they behave is the end product both of the conditions under which they were reared and of their constitution, their intellect, temperament, and personality.

In seeking the answer to the question why some children develop a tendency to antisocial behavior while others manage to comply with the rules of society and law, one often begins with a study of intelligence or personality traits. Yet these characteristics do not express themselves in a human vacuum. They are at least partially anchored in bodily constitution. They are not all due to life's experiences. The bodily constitution is, moreover, not only basic but first in point of time in the history of an individual.

While it is risky to generalize about the exact participation of heredity and environment in the end product of human personality and character, this much can safely be said: bodily constitution embraces the more fixed and permanent core of the human being (anatomically and physiologically). In essential structure it is probably genetically determined, although affected, also, by early (intra- or extra-uterine) environmental influences.

The questions to be answered by this portion of the re-

search are: Do delinquents differ in physique from nondelinquents? And, if so, how?

As a basis for the inquiry, full-length photographs (front,
side, rear) of the 500 delinquents and 500 nondelinquents
were taken.[1] These were turned over to a physical anthropologist (Carl C. Seltzer of Harvard University) who examined each photograph to determine by methods which he
devised (1) gross bodily measurements, (2) various bodily
indices and disproportions, (3) the relative presence or absence of what is called by anthropologists "gynandromorphy"
or the "masculinity component," and (4) most important, the
general bodily pattern or *somatotype*.

Before considering the findings, the reader is again reminded that delinquents and nondelinquents were matched
at the outset in accordance with their ethnic origins (Italian
for Italian, Irish for Irish, Greek for Greek, and so on). This
precludes the possibility that any differences in the physique
of delinquents and nondelinquents are due to differences in
their racial stock.[2]

Gross Bodily Measurements

Detailed comparisons of many *gross bodily measurements*
of the delinquent boys with the nondelinquents consistently
brought out differences, usually revealing a significant superiority of the former over the latter. In eight of sixteen major
measurements the delinquents show significant excess: in
neck breadth, shoulder breadth, chest breadth, distance between nipples, breadth and depth of waist, and forearm and
upper arm breadth. The delinquents are, however, narrower

[1] For detailed method of taking the photographs and of analyzing them,
see *Unraveling Juvenile Delinquency*, Appendix C, p. 307, prepared by Carl
C. Seltzer.

[2] For method of determining the ethnic origin of the delinquents and the
nondelinquents, see *Unraveling Juvenile Delinquency*, pp. 32, 33.

in face breadth. They have some tendency, also, to narrower hips and smaller lower limbs.

On the whole, although the differences in bodily measurements between the delinquents and the nondelinquents are not great, the delinquents, far from being inferior in physique to nondelinquents, are actually somewhat superior.

Even these simple metric differences already begin to suggest that the delinquents tend to form the physical outline of the athletic, "mesomorphic" type, as shown by the generally greater breadth of their bodies, broader shoulders, and more muscular arms.

Another important point emerged from comparison of the delinquents with the nondelinquents in respect to gross bodily dimensions: quite typically, the lawbreakers remained inferior to the nondelinquents in their bodily measurements until their thirteenth or fourteenth year, at which time a *growth spurt* occurred during which the delinquents not only caught up with, but in some respects surpassed, the nondelinquents. The difference in their average dimensions between the thirteenth and the fourteenth year was found to be greater among the delinquents than among the nondelinquents in fifteen out of sixteen bodily measurements. If the impression is prevalent that juvenile delinquents are small and "underslung," we see now that it is because their growth is retarded until the thirteenth to fourteenth year. This is a striking point of distinction between the delinquents and the law-abiding boys, and may well signify some fundamental physiologic-endocrinologic differences between the two which are perhaps related to energy output.

Comparison of the gross bodily measurements of the 500 delinquents and their 500 matched nondelinquents has thus revealed two important facts—that delinquents are superior to nondelinquents in their bodily measurements and that they spurt in their growth in the thirteenth to fourteenth year after a slower physical development than characterizes the nondelinquents.

Bodily Indices and Disproportions

More significant than gross bodily dimensions, however, is a check on how the two sets of boys compare in respect to various bodily *indices* or ratios. These are associations between two bodily measurements. A series of them can be especially revealing in sizing up both general bodily types and specific bodily disproportions.

Two sets of such cross-reference measurements were made: those relating various lateral bodily spans with each other and those relating lateral measurements to stature. In seventeen[3] out of twenty-one of the former, significant differences were revealed between the two groups. For example, in relation to their hip breadth, the delinquents were found to have deeper and broader chests, wider shoulders, and greater waist breadth than the nondelinquents. Relative to shoulder and chest breadth, the delinquents have narrower faces than the control group. In relation to the breadth of their thighs, waist, chest, and shoulders, the former have smaller calves than the latter. The differentiating indices are such as to confirm the earlier-mentioned outline of the delinquents as tending, on the whole, to a closely knit, muscular pattern with broad shoulders and tapering torso, the hallmarks of the mesomorphic constitutional type.

Lateral measurements related to *stature* once more reveal a predominantly mesomorphic constitutional pattern among the delinquents, accompanied by a pronounced lack of the ectomorphic (linear, fragile) component.[4] In eleven of fifteen tie-ins of various bodily dimensions with height, significant

[3] See *Unraveling*, pp. 188-189, 316-325.
[4] See *Unraveling*, pp. 189-190, 325-334.

differences emerged between delinquents and nondelinquents, revealing an appreciably greater laterality (broadness) of body build among the former. For example, relative to stature, the delinquents have broader necks, chests, shoulders, waists, thighs, upper extremities. Again, the mesomorphic, athletic outline emerges, in the proportionately broader neck, shoulders, chest and waist, the more muscular forearm, and the tapering torso. There is a greater stockiness of build among the delinquents as contrasted with greater linearity or slenderness among the nondelinquents.

All the delinquent boys do not of course always contrast as markedly with the nondelinquents as is shown by the analysis of averages; but there do exist statistically significant differences between the two groups taken as a whole, which tend to emphasize the mesomorphy of the delinquents.

Another aspect of this portion of the anthropologic inquiry was designed to show *bodily disproportions*. These may be of importance, not merely as an indication of possible disharmony of physique but also as perhaps indicating disharmony on a physiologic-temperamental level. (We are at present exploring some aspects of this possibility.) By disproportion is meant a substantial divergence from the average in respect to certain restricted ranges of bodily ratios, such as excessive head size in relation to the size of the chest; excessive narrowness of chest in relation to width of shoulders; and the like.[5] Analysis of the two sets of boys from this point of view shows that in all ten bodily areas investigated,[6] with the exception of very narrow legs in relation to width of shoulders, the delinquent group is more harmonious or less disproportionate in physique than the nondelinquent. For example, the delinquents are less disproportioned than

[5] The method of determining extreme disharmony of physique (and all other aspects of the anthropometric study) is described by Seltzer in Appendix C of *Unraveling*.

[6] See *Unraveling*, pp. 191-192, 334-339.

the nondelinquents in their stature as related to their body weight, and in the breadth of their faces in relation to their chest width. These differences were found to be essentially independent of age.

It has thus become evident that the delinquents are more harmoniously organized for direct physical activity, probably making easier the conversion of impulse into action.

Masculine Component

In terms of *masculinity* (the extent to which a boy is characterized by angular, narrow-hipped, rough-surfaced, well-muscled characteristics usually associated with the male, rather than the rounder, softer, broader-hipped, less well-muscled feminine type), a strong masculine component was found to exist in the great majority of the physiques of *both* sets of boys. Nevertheless, weakness in this virile element, small in both groups, is only about a fourth as great among the delinquents as among the nondelinquents (2%:8%).

Classification into Body Types

Apart from the specific, minute measurements of dimensions and ratios, two complementary methods were employed by Seltzer for arriving at a reliable classification of the delinquents and nondelinquents into *bodily (morphologic) types:* (a) On the basis of inspection of the photographs, a somatotype rating was made. (b) A matched-pair comparison of each delinquent and each nondelinquent was separately made, to determine how each member of a pair differed from his "opposite number."[7] (Both methods of analysis of the photographs are described in detail on pp. 192-194 and 340-347 of

[7] This matched-pair comparison was made by Carl C. Seltzer; the over-all inspectional somatotype ratings previously discussed were made by Ashton M. Tenney.

Juvenile Delinquency.) As a result of these two independent series of analyses of the physiques of the 500 delinquents and 500 nondelinquents, a somatotype classification in terms of the predominance of one of three constitutional components—*endomorphy* (softness, roundness), *mesomorphy* (predominance of muscle, bone, and connective tissue), and *ectomorphy* (linearity, fragility of body build)—can be safely accepted as a reliable assessment.

Each of these three somatotypes contains subtypes, the existence of pure endomorphy, mesomorphy or ectomorphy being rare. Each physique (with the exception of the "extreme" type) has within it distinguishable elements of each of the three major somatotypes in varying proportions, which a thoroughly competent physical anthropologist can determine. And he can also determine which one of the three somatotype characteristics predominates in each particular physique.

As a result of the dual analysis of the photographs, it was found, first, that, although the total number of endomorphs (those of soft, round physique) is small in our sample of 500 delinquents and 500 nondelinquents, the incidence of endomorphic predominance is hardly lower among the delinquents than among the nondelinquents (12%:15%). It is in the *dominance of mesomorphy by which the delinquents as a group are most highly characterized, and in which they far exceed the nondelinquents* (60%:31%).

As regards the predominance of *ectomorphy* (linearity and fragility) in the physiques of delinquents and nondelinquents, this exists in far *lower* proportion among the former (14%:40%).

There is also among the delinquents and nondelinquents a group of *balanced* physiques, those in which each of the three constitutional components (soft-roundness, muscularity, linearity) occur in equal proportion (14%:15%).

The most striking difference, therefore, in the physiques of delinquents and nondelinquents is in the element of mesomorphy (muscularity). The existence of *subtypes* in both groups, in which the marked participation of other constitutional elements is evident, should not be overlooked, however. The interested reader is referred to *Unraveling Juvenile Delinquency,* Table XV-1, pp. 193, 343, for details.

Comparison of the physiques of 500 delinquents and 500 nondelinquents has disclosed a number of significant findings that cannot be ignored in any comprehensive analysis of the causal factors involved in delinquency. First, as a group the law-violating boys have *sturdier bodies* than the law-abiding ones. Secondly, their body structure is *more harmonious.* Thirdly, they are somewhat more *masculine.* Most important, if we reflect on the findings regarding bodily indices and physique types (the latter derived by two independent means), we are forced to the striking conclusion that the majority of *persistent juvenile delinquents are typically of the mesomorphic, muscular, well-knit athletic type.*

Thus, when tracing the evolution of personality and the root tendencies to antisocial or socially acceptable behavior, we must take into account constitutional endowment along with the early influences surrounding the child in home, school, and neighborhood. Constitutional equipment tends to determine whether the stream of life will on the whole be powerful, tempestuous, turbulent; or will meander placidly; or will flow rigid in straight and narrow banks. But whether the life current will flood its shores and cause serious social harm depends in large measure upon the environmental-cultural terrain through which it flows.

Of course, the relationship of body types to motivations, attitudes, and behavior tendencies has not been clarified. The fact that a boy has an essentially mesomorphic constitution

seems very remote from the fact that he is a persistent delinquent. We are at present engaged in detailed intercorrelations
of various body types with numerous factors of personality,
character, and social "conditioning" processes. A great deal
of information that we would have liked to place before the
reader in this book must await the outcome of such exploration.

CHAPTER X

Health and Delinquency

No clinical study of a delinquent is deemed complete without a physical examination. However, the reason for requiring exploration into the health of the maladjusted youth is not always clear. It is obvious that there may be endocrinologic and other deficiencies related to symptoms of fatigue, irritability, and the like, or sensory or muscular handicaps, which have not only a physiologic but a psychologic significance for attitude and behavior. Apart from this, the frequently mentioned "inferiority complex" with its compensatory reaction phenomena may be significant in analyzing the roots of maladjustment and delinquency.

The possible threads of causation in the field of physical ill-health and handicap are much more difficult to trace and unravel, because they are much less directly related to attitudes, motivations, and behavior tendencies than are those in some of the other areas of this research.

There is a popular notion that juvenile delinquents are on the whole a less healthy group of youngsters than are non-delinquents. It was our major purpose in the medical examination to determine whether or not this is a fact and to see in what ways delinquents and nondelinquents actually do differ in their physical condition.

Scope of Health Examination

It was the consensus of the experts who advised us that a standard, systematic medical examination for the purpose of comparing the general health of the delinquents and their matched nondelinquents would be sufficient for our purposes and should result in the revelation of possible areas for deeper exploration in a later research.

The height and weight of each boy was taken. Abnormalities of his bony skeleton and palate were recorded. Teeth were examined for imperfect development, crowding, and cavities; nose and throat, for enlarged or diseased tonsils, obstructed nares, and ailments of the upper respiratory system. Eyes were examined for defects, such as strabismus, nystagmus, myopia, hyperopia, and astigmatism; eye injuries and left-eyedness also were noted. Ears were examined for deafness and otitis media, and attention was given to any other obvious sensory defects. Examination was made of the heart, the lungs, the abdomen (with particular reference to appendectomy and hernia), and the genital organs. Skin conditions were noted, such as dermatitis, eczema, psoriasis, acne, and impetigo; so also were glandular disturbances of the lymph, thyroid, pituitary, and sex glands. A brief neurological examination gave particular attention to irregular reflexes (pupillary, abdominal, cremasteric, and patellar), dermographia, cyanosis, and tremors. Functional deviations were noted, particularly stuttering, lisping, tics, extreme nailbiting, and left-handedness; and motor handicaps originating from disease or accident were recorded. Finally, an estimate was made by the examining physician of the present health status of each boy.

The physician who carried out all the examinations, both in

the correctional schools and in the public schools (Dr. Bryant
E. Moulton), has suggested that the delinquent boys, being
confined in correctional institutions, might be found to be in
better physical condition in certain respects than the nondelinquents because of the attention given in the institutions
to their nutrition and to remediable defects. This possibility
must be borne in mind. However, most of the physical conditions about which data were sought are not subject to
change by a few months' stay in a correctional institution; for
example, pathology of the bony skeleton and palate, imperfectly developed and crowded teeth, obstructed nares, visual
and auditory defects, cardiac disease and impairment of pulmonary function (tuberculosis and asthma), genital pathology, certain skin pathology, glandular disturbances (with the
possible exception of disturbances of lymph glands), acquired
motor handicaps, neurological handicaps, and functional
deviations (with the possible exception of stuttering).

Developmental Health History

Before proceeding to the findings of the medical examination, we present some facts in the early health history of the
boys which have been derived from interviews with their
mothers, often supplemented by medical and social agency
reports. We were especially interested to determine whether
the mother's pregnancy with the boy was uneventful, whether
he was instrumentally delivered or malformed at birth,
whether he was born prematurely or was much underweight
at birth, whether he had convulsions or spasms in infancy,
serious accidents or operations, whether he was unduly retarded in walking or talking, and, in general, whether he was
sickly as an infant.

Only relatively small numbers of both groups of boys were

characterized by any of these conditions. With the exception of the fact that somewhat more of the delinquents than the nondelinquents (15%:10%) are reported to have been sickly babies—that is, cranky, fretful, nervous, or irritable—the delinquents and the nondelinquents closely resemble each other.

Information was sought from some adult member of the boy's family (usually his mother or mother substitute) about certain aspects of his health beyond infancy, such as specific susceptibilities (recurrent colds of the head or chest, ear defects, digestive disturbances, allergic phenomena) or a history of enuresis or extreme restlessness. Although we sought many more facts concerning the boys' developmental history, we found that the memories of our informants were often vague and that, in connection with these and other early health data, insufficient information was elicited on which to base sound judgments. However, some of the data for which substantiation was derived from other sources are revealing.

As regards susceptibility to disturbances of various kinds, there appears to be little difference between delinquents and nondelinquents in the extent to which they suffered from recurrent colds of the head or chest; had ear difficulties (earaches, mastoid, middle-ear infections, and the like); suffered from digestive disturbances; or were prone to allergic phenomena (skin troubles, asthma, hay fever, and so forth). However, the informants reported double the proportion of delinquents as of nondelinquents (60%:30%) as having been *extremely restless children,* unable to sit still, always wanting "to be on the go," and as having been enuretic well beyond the age when bladder control is normally established (28%: 14%). Whether this greater restlessness and enuresis are largely the results of physiologic-temperamental constitution or are essentially psychosomatic reactive phenomena, we cannot determine at the present stage. When we come to relate these factors to physique types and Rorschach Test (in a subsequent volume), we may be able to throw more light on the matter. Meanwhile these findings seem to lend strength to the probability that even in early childhood the delinquents were more "difficult" than the nondelinquents.

Immunity to Contagion

The social investigators also questioned the families about the frequency and severity of the usual childhood contagious diseases (measles, chicken pox, whooping cough, mumps, scarlet fever, diphtheria) in order to determine a boy's resistance to such ailments. In instances in which there was no record of contagious diseases, the boy was judged to have *good* immunity; where some contagious diseases had occurred, but in mild form, his immunity was described as *fair;* and in cases in which contagious diseases were frequent or severe ("Johnny was very sick; I thought he would die"), his resistance was described as *poor.* The results of this inquiry revealed no significant difference between the delinquents and the nondelinquents in their immunity to contagious disease.

Height and Weight

A close similarity was found in the average height of the delinquent and the nondelinquent group (62:62.4 inches).

As regards weight, there is likewise not too much difference between the two groups, the average weight of the delinquent boys being 112 pounds and of the nondelinquent boys, 109 pounds. Although it might on the surface appear that the somewhat greater average weight of the delinquents as a group is due to the fact that they have been institutionalized and gained weight because of better feeding than they might have had at home, a breakdown of the two groups by age classes as related to weight does not seem to justify this supposition. The delinquents are lighter than the nondelinquents in the age classes up to and including the fourteen-year group, but the older delinquents (those who are fifteen years and over) are heavier than their comparable nondelinquents. Since the younger offenders do not exceed the nondelinquents in weight, it cannot be concluded that the possibly better diet in the correctional schools has anything to do with the somewhat greater average weight of the delinquents as a whole (see Chapter IX regarding growth spurt of the delinquents).

Bony Skeleton and Palate

Any evidence of lesion or faulty development of the bony skeleton was recorded by the examining physician. No essential difference between delinquents and nondelinquents was revealed.

Each boy was examined for deviations in the continuity or shape of the hard, bony palate. No greater proportion of palatal abnormalities was found among the delinquents than among the nondelinquents.

Attention was directed to the Lombrosian stigmata of narrowness and breadth of palate, prognathism (projecting jaws), high or low arching, and cleft palate. Although the extent of palatal abnormalities is no greater among the delinquents than among the nondelinquents, two minor differences between the two groups were uncovered, namely, a *lower* proportion of the delinquents have prognathous jaws, and a larger proportion have low-arched palates. The first finding is of particular interest in view of the Lombrosian conception held by many persons that criminals typically have jutting jaws.

Teeth

Examination of the mouth was concerned, first, with imperfectly developed teeth, that is, dentition evidencing some severe interference with normal development, in contrast with carious teeth. No difference was found in this respect between delinquents and nondelinquents.

Likewise in regard to crowding of teeth (recorded only when there was an obvious disparity between the size of the upper or lower jaw and the room required by the teeth), very slight difference was found.

In regard to dental caries, the examining physician recorded carious teeth only when several caries were present or had been present, as evidenced by many fillings. On this basis, likewise, the delinquents and the nondelinquents closely resemble each other.

Nose and Throat

Examination of the nose and throat was directed toward the presence of enlarged or diseased tonsils, obstructed nares, and pathology of the upper respiratory system.

The tonsils were examined for any increase in size or any distinct evidence of infection detectable by visual examination. Again, no difference was discernible between delinquents and nondelinquents.

Note was made of any structural constriction of the nasal passages, usually due to a deviated septum but more rarely caused by some hypertrophy of the soft tissue (polyps, enlarged turbinates, and so on). And here also delinquents and nondelinquents were found to resemble each other.

No difference exists between the two groups in pathology

of the nose and throat and accessory sinuses, such as sinusitis, pharyngitis, laryngitis, or rhinitis (inflammation of nasal mucous membranes).

Eyes and Ears

Each delinquent and nondelinquent was examined for eye and ear defects that were sufficiently serious to interfere observably with his social adjustment.

In the examination of the eyes, those conditions which can be easily recognized without special optical equipment were noted, such as strabismus (a condition in which the visual axes fail to meet at the objective point because of incoordination of the eye muscles); nystagmus (an involuntary oscillatory movement of the eyeballs); and visual defects commonly encountered in adolescence, such as myopia (nearsightedness), hyperopia (farsightedness), and marked astigmatism (defect in which rays of light from a point do not converge to a point on the retina). Examination was also made for left-eyedness. The ears were examined especially for deafness and otitis media (inflammation of the middle ear). Summarizing all these eye and ear defects, it was found that there is no greater proportion of their incidence among the delinquents than among the nondelinquents, slightly over half of each group having one or more visual or aural handicaps.

Heart and Lungs

In the examination of the chest any significant pathological condition of the heart, as indicated by unusual size or location of the heart or unusual heart sounds, was noted; and, again, no statistically valid difference was found between the two groups in the presence of readily detectable heart ailments.

Significant pathological conditions of the lungs, as determined by external physical examination, such as tuberculosis, asthma, and bronchitis, were also noted. Here likewise little or no difference was discovered between the two groups of boys.

Abdomen and Genitalia

Physical examination of the abdomen was made for evidence of appendectomy and for the presence of hernia. Operations for appendicitis have taken place (as shown by operative scars) among equally small proportions of the delinquents and nondelinquents, and there was evidence of hernia (defined as an abnormal patency existing in the muscular wall of the abdomen—inguinal, femoral, or ventral) in small and equal proportions of both groups.

In the examination of the genitalia, any marked deviation in the anatomical structure or evidence of any pathological process was recorded. Here, again, there is a marked resemblance between delinquents and nondelinquents, a fifth of each group having malformations or pathology of one sort or another, including undescended testes, underdeveloped testes, phimosis (constriction of preputial opening), and other genital malformations.

Skin

The physician observed such skin conditions as dermatitis (inflammation of skin), eczema (inflammation with exudation of lymph), psoriasis (a chronic skin disease with scale formation), acne (inflammation of oil glands), and impetigo (an acute pustular skin inflammation). Pathology of the skin was not found to exist in any greater degree among the delinquents than among the nondelinquents.

Glands

For the purposes of this examination, attention was given only to those glandular disturbances which are externally observable. Here the physician was looking for enlarged lymph glands, thyroid and pituitary disturbances, and over- and under-development of the sex glands. Such glandular disturbances were found to exist in equally low proportions among the delinquents and the nondelinquents.[1]

Nervous System

Each boy was examined for exaggerated and diminished reflexes, for dermographia, cyanosis, tremors, and any other neurological signs that might indicate some defect of the nervous system.

The reflexes with which the physician was especially concerned are pupillary, abdominal, cremasteric (testicular), and patellar (knee jerk), and he recorded any marked deviation from the accepted norm of deep or superficial reflexes, the presence of which may or may not be of diagnostic significance. It was found that irregular reflexes occur in about equal proportion among delinquents and nondelinquents.

As to other neurological handicaps, with the exception of dermographia (an hysteric condition in which tracings may be made on the skin), no observable difference was noted between the two groups: cyanosis (blue discoloration of skin from nonoxidation of blood), tremors, and so on. Dermographia was found to be less marked among the delinquents than among the nondelinquents (45%:58%). The lower incidence of neurological conditions among the delinquents

[1] In interpreting these findings, it must be remembered that the physical examination was limited to observations by a highly experienced physician, without, however, including laboratory procedures.

as reflected in the finding concerning dermographia is possibly related to the fact that a lower proportion of delinquents than of the nondelinquents have psychoneurotic characteristics.

Summarizing all the neurological findings, there is a difference in the proportion of delinquents and nondelinquents evidencing neurological handicaps of one sort or another.[2] Although such signs exist in large numbers among both groups, they are present to a less extent among the delinquents (64%:73%). Again, this is probably related to the greater proportion of nondelinquents having psychoneurotic characteristics, as revealed in later chapters by the Rorschach Test and the psychiatric findings (Chapters XII, XIII, and XIV).

In the matter of functional deviations (that is, observable persistent divergencies from normal behavior, ordinarily not known to be directly related to specific organic pathology), attention was given to stuttering, lisping, tics, extreme nailbiting, left-handedness, and ambidexterity. A summary of the evidences of such clear functional deviations as were noted in the physical examination shows that delinquents and nondelinquents display one or another of the defects in question in remarkably *similar* proportions (41%:40%).

In examining the nature of these functional deviations more closely, however, it is seen that a significantly *lower* proportion of the delinquents than of the nondelinquents have tics (3%:8%) and are ambidextrous (1%:5%). Extreme nailbiting was found more frequently among the delinquents (21.4%:15.6%).

Acquired Motor Handicaps

The examining physician's attention was directed toward any impairment of strength or of motion, whether due to

[2] Other classifications of neurological handicaps and of functional deviations are, of course, possible; we have followed the arrangement set up by Dr. Moulton.

paralysis of muscle or nerve or to faulty structure of the skeletal apparatus (bones, joints, connective tissue). Equally small proportions of both groups of boys were found to have motor handicaps. Among seven of twelve delinquents motor handicaps were the result of accident rather than of disease, and this pertains likewise to ten of sixteen nondelinquents.

General Health

With the completion of each examination the physician made a judgment as to the presence of defects and their permanency and gravity. Remediable defects are those "which should in all probability clear up or be negated under conventional medical treatment." Irremediable defects are those "for which conventional medical treatment appears to offer little hope of amelioration."

Various kinds of defects, although numerous in both groups, were found to be present in significantly lower proportion among the delinquents than among the nondelinquents (63%:75%). Also a lesser number of the delinquents were found to have remediable defects. This can be largely, perhaps entirely, explained by the fact that they have already had the benefit of medical attention in correctional institutions. However, almost as many of the delinquents as of the nondelinquents are suffering from irremediable defects, which would seem to indicate that in this respect there is little, if any, difference in the general health status of the two groups.

The above observation is confirmed by the estimate made by the physician of the general health of the boys. This is described as *excellent* if a boy's general development is sound, if he is well nourished, and has no defects; *good* if he has minor defects, which are, however, not disabling; *fair* if his health is below par in general development and nutrition, regardless of whether he has defects that are partially disabling; and *poor* if he has definite physical handicaps and/or disabling defects.

From this skilled medical estimate the view that delinquents are in poorer health than boys whose behavior is not antisocial receives no support. Fifteen per cent of the delinquents and nondelinquents are graded as in "excellent" health; 77% of the delinquents and 73% of the nondelinquents in "good" health; 7% of the delinquents and 11% of the nondelinquents in "fair" health; and 1% of the delinquents and 1% of the nondelinquents in "poor" health.

In arriving at the general health status, the physician took account of the nutritional development of the boys to the extent that it could be determined by an experienced medical observer who has long specialized in the examination of youngsters. Since the boys whose general health is found to be excellent or good are those who are well nourished, it follows that quite similar proportions of both delinquents and nondelinquents were found to be well nourished.

Summarizing the findings of the medical examination of the delinquents and the nondelinquents, we see that *the view that delinquents are in poorer health than nondelinquents is not justified. Little, if any, difference exists between the physical condition of the two groups as a whole.*

First, as regards their health as infants and young children, no differences between the two sets of boys have been revealed from careful inquiry of their mothers and consultation of early medical records, except for the two important facts that a considerably higher proportion of the delinquents are reported to have been *enuretic and extremely restless children.* As regards their susceptibilities to disease and infection and their immunity to contagious diseases, they resemble each other.

Certain differences emerging from the medical examination are worth stressing:

Although there is no over-all difference between the two

groups as regards palatal abnormalities, a significantly lower proportion of the delinquents have prognathous jaws (believed to be a frequently found characteristic of the "criminal type"), and a significantly higher proportion have low-arched palates, though the numbers involved here are small.

A significantly *lower* proportion of the delinquents than of the nondelinquents have neurological handicaps.

Although there is no over-all difference between the two groups in observable evidences of functional deviations, a few differences in the incidence of certain of these deviations should be recalled: tics and ambidexterity are less prevalent among the delinquents, while extreme nailbiting is more characteristic of the delinquents, although this latter does not quite reach the level of statistical significance. The first two differences may be associated with the fact already noted that a lower proportion of the delinquents have neurotic characteristics, in general; and the latter difference with the probability that, in greater measure than the control group, the delinquents tend to be of the oral-erotic type (see later chapters).

CHAPTER XI

Intelligence and Delinquency

For a long time it was taken for granted that mental defect, especially outright feeble-mindedness, was a chief cause of juvenile delinquency. More recently, however, it has become apparent that deficiency of intellect is not among the more important characteristics of delinquents. The earlier emphasis on this factor of intellectual defect is a good illustration of what happens when it is concluded that a trait which seems to occur frequently among delinquents necessarily indicates that they deviate in that respect from nondelinquents. Only by resort to comparison of the group under scrutiny with a control group of true nondelinquents can valid conclusions be drawn.

It will be recalled that at the very outset of our inquiry we matched the 500 persistently misbehaving boys with the 500 law-abiding ones in respect to *general,* or "global," intelligence. The 500 matched pairs encompassed a wide range of intelligence quotients. For example, 140 of the delinquents and 152 of the nondelinquents had an I.Q. of 100 or over on the Wechsler-Bellevue Full Scale Intelligence Test; at the other end of the scale, 359 of the former and 346 of the latter ranged downward in I.Q. from 99 to 60. The *average intelligence quotient* of the two groups proved to be 92 among the delinquents and 94 in the control group. The reader will agree with Dr. David Wechsler, the originator of the test, that this is indeed a close matching of the two sets of boys.

It remains now to find out whether the various *specific skills and abilities* that enter into the composition of global intelligence are similar among delinquents and nondelinquents. We are, therefore, concerned here with presenting the findings regarding the *components* of general intelligence, which were largely determined through the Wechsler-Bellevue Test and in part by the Rorschach Test.

Wechsler-Bellevue Test

The Wechsler-Bellevue Test, which consists of a Vocabulary test and five Verbal subtests (Information, Similarities, Comprehension, Arithmetic Reasoning, and Memory Span for Digits) and five Performance subtests (Digit Symbol, Picture Completion, Picture Arrangement, Block Design, and Object Assembly) divides general intelligence into Verbal and Performance.

The *Verbal* aspect of the intellectual process deals with the use of abstract intelligence—that is, such matters as the extent of vocabulary, information, ability to discern similarities, to comprehend problems intellectually, to carry on the kind of logical reasoning involved in the solving of arithmetical problems, and the employment of the memory in immediate recall of a series of numbers. Experience has shown that these different intellectual processes are among the basic ones in thinking and reasoning.

The *Performance* aspect of the Wechsler-Bellevue Test deals more with what might be called "practical intelligence" or "hand-mindedness." The subtests in this portion of the Wechsler-Bellevue Scale are designed to disclose the kind of intellectual activity that is involved in the handling of concrete materials rather than abstract ideas.

On the total verbal quotient the delinquents make a slightly poorer showing than the nondelinquents (89:92); but the groups resemble each other closely in the average of their performance intelligence quotient (97:98).

When, however, we looked into the scores on the *individual* subtests of the Verbal and Performance scales, significant differences began to appear between the delinquents and the nondelinquents.

Verbal Intelligence

The delinquents show less aptitude in the *Vocabulary, Information,* and *Comprehension* tests, although they tend to resemble the nondelinquents in scores obtained on the *Similarities Test, Arithmetical Reasoning,* and *Memory Span for Digits.* The differences are small, but statistical computation shows them to be truly significant and not due merely to chance. (The reader interested in the exact figures is invited to consult *Unraveling,* p. 199.)

To realize the implications of these findings we ought to consider what Dr. Wechsler, the originator of the test, has to say about these various aspects of intelligence.

First, as to *Vocabulary,* he tells us that it is a highly important clue to general mental capacity: "The size of a man's vocabulary is not only an index of his schooling, but also an excellent measure of his general intelligence. Its excellence as a test of intelligence is seemingly derived from the fact that the number of words a man knows is at once a measure of his learning ability, his fund of verbal information, and of the general range of his ideas." (Wechsler, *The Measurement of Adult Intelligence,* 3d ed. 1944, pp. 98-99.)

In regard to the significance of the *Information* test, "all objections allowed for, the range of a man's knowledge is generally a very good indication of his intellectual capacity." (Wechsler, pp. 77-80.)

In respect to the implications of the *Comprehension* test,

Wechsler says that "offhand it might be termed a test of common sense. . . Success on the test seemingly depends on the possession of a certain amount of practical information and a general ability to evaluate past experience. . . Indeed, when given to children, the answers to these questions show a considerable correlation with age and social maturity." (Wechsler, p. 81.)

Information as to the significance of the subtests of the *Verbal* battery (*Similarities, Arithmetic Reasoning,* and *Memory Span for Digits*), in which little difference was found between the two sets of boys, is given in the footnote.[1]

There are, then, clear deficiencies among delinquents in certain constituents of abstract intelligence; namely, vocabulary, information, and comprehension. However, even these differences between them and the nondelinquents may not indicate any completely innate dissimilarity in intellectual power between the two groups. Environmental circumstances are doubtless also involved. The Vocabulary test, although a good indicator of general intellectual capacity, is partially affected by the amount of schooling; and we have seen (Chapter VII) that the delinquents truanted excessively and were more retarded in school than the nondelinquents. The Information test, although likewise a good indicator of intel-

[1] "The [Similarities] test has certain qualitative features, the most important of which is the light which the type of responses received throws upon the logical character of the subject's thinking processes. There is an obvious difference both as to maturity and as to level of thinking between the individual who says that a banana and an orange are alike because they both have a skin, and the individual who says that they are both fruit."—Wechsler, pp. 86-87.

"Arithmetical Reasoning tests correlate highly with global measures of intelligence," and "children who do poorly in arithmetical reasoning have difficulty with other subjects."—Wechsler, p. 82.

"Memory span, whether for digits forwards or backwards, correlates very poorly with all other tests of intelligence. The ability involved contains little of 'g' [general intelligence factor], and. . . is more or less independent of the general factor. . .The failure to repeat digits backwards does often correlate with difficulties of attention and lack of ability in doing intellectual work which requires concentrated effort. . .This deficiency is often referred to by psychologists as lack of mental control."—Wechsler, pp. 83-84.

lectual grasp, is also considerably affected by educational opportunities (not merely in school but in the home) as well as by the cultural atmosphere of the household. It will be re-called (Chapter VI) that in the latter respect the delinquents were considerably less advantaged than the nondelinquents. Success on the Comprehension test, on the other hand, depends not only on possession of practical information but on the ability to evaluate past experience; and in this test poor verbalizers (as the delinquents are) tend to make lower scores.

Performance Intelligence

Turning now to the subtests of the *Performance* aspect of the Wechsler-Bellevue Scale, a comparison of the accomplish-ments of the boys in this form of intellectual endeavor shows that, although the delinquents have slightly less aptitude than the other boys on the *Digit Symbol* test, they have a little more ability than the nondelinquents on the *Block Design* and *Object Assembly* tests. However, the two groups resemble each other in their scores on the *Picture Completion* and the *Picture Arrangement* tests. (See *Unraveling*, p. 202.)

What is the meaning of these test findings?

In the *Digit Symbol* test (in which the delinquents are *deficient*), "the subject is required to associate certain symbols with certain other symbols, and the speed and accuracy with which he does it serve as a measure of his intellectual ability .....Neurotic and unstable individuals also tend to do rather badly on the Digit Symbol test. . .because they have difficulty in concentrating and applying themselves for any length of time and because of their emotional reactivity to any task requiring persistent effort. The poor performance of the neurotic represents a lessened mental efficiency rather than an impairment of intellectual ability." (Wechsler, pp. 94, 95.)

The *Block Design* test (in which the delinquents were found to do *better* than the other boys) "in some way involves both synthetic and analytical ability. . .One can often distinguish the hasty and impulsive individual from the deliberate and careful type, a subject who gives up easily or gets disgusted, from the one who persists and keeps on working even after his time is up, and so on of a number of other temperamental traits which manifest themselves not infrequently in the course of a subject's performance." (Wechsler, pp. 92-93.) Yet, contrary to what might be expected in accordance with other aspects of this research in which it has been found that the delinquents are more impulsive, they scored better on the whole than the nondelinquents on this test.

The *Object Assembly* test (in which, also, the delinquents' performance was somewhat better than the nondelinquents') presents the problem of assembling the parts of "three separate figure formboards, a Manikin, a Feature Profile, and a Hand." The best feature of this test is "its qualitative merits." Various examiners have praised the test repeatedly, because "it tells you something about the thinking and working habits of the subjects. The subjects' approach to the task may in fact be one of several kinds. The first is that of an immediate reaction to the whole, accompanied by a critical understanding of the relation of the individual parts. . .A second type of response is that of rapid recognition of the whole but with imperfect understanding of the relations between the parts. . .Still a third type. . . is one which may start with complete failure to take in the total situation, but which after a certain amount of trial and error manifestation leads to a sudden though often belated appreciation of the figure. . . The Object Assembly test has a particular clinical value because it tells us something about one's mode of perception, the degree to which one relies on trial and error methods, and the manner in which one reacts to mistakes."[2]

Information regarding the significance of those subtests of

[2] However, the Object Assembly test has one weak feature: it "shows the smallest correlation with all other tests when taken individually or collectively." (Wechsler, pp. 97-98.)

the Performance battery (*Picture Completion* and *Picture Arrangement*), in which little difference was found between the two sets of boys, is given in the footnote.[3]

It is clear from this analysis of the components of "hand-minded" intelligence that the delinquents appear to have less speed and accuracy than the nondelinquents in associating certain symbols with others (Digit Symbol test); but they perform better than the controls on the Object Assembly and Block Design tests.

In assaying the differences in these aspects of performance intelligence we must bear in mind the fact that the *Digit Symbol test,* on which the delinquents scored *less* than the control group, involves concentration and persistency of effort and is therefore a test in which impulsive, emotionally labile persons would not perform as effectively as those who are more stable. (It will be seen later that the delinquents are on the whole more impulsive emotionally than the nondelinquents.) As to the slight superiority of the former over the latter in the *Block Design* and *Object Assembly* tests, this may reflect a greater native skill in motor capacity, a quality not without use in certain forms of delinquent behavior, such as "snitching" things in ten-cent stores, stealing cars, burglary, and so on.

The reader will probably agree that, on the whole, the differences between the delinquents and the controls in respect

[3] "The ability of an individual to do this [Picture Completion Test] depends in a large measure upon his relative familiarity with the object with which he is presented, that is to say, upon the actual content of the picture. A person who has never seen or read about a steamship cannot be expected to know that all such boats have funnels and that these are generally to be found at the center of the ship."—Wechsler, p. 91.

The Picture Arrangement test "consists of a series of pictures which, when placed in the right sequence, tell a little story. . .The pictures are presented to the subject in a disarranged order and he is asked to put them together in the right order so that they make a sensible story. . .The. . .test effectively measures a subject's ability to comprehend and size up a total situation. . .the subject matter of the test nearly always involves some human or practical situation."—Wechsler, pp. 87-89.

to the details of intellectual capacity, although not marked, assume significance by the very fact that the two sets of boys were matched at the outset in respect to their global intelligence.

It appears to be a fact that *the antisocial boys are somewhat superior to the law-abiding ones in those types of intellectual tasks in which the approach to meaning or significance is by direct physical relationships (Block Design, Object Assembly) with but slight dependence on a system of intermediary symbols. The delinquents do not accumulate as large a system of symbols (Vocabulary test) or of symbolized informational content (Information test). Their generalizations are more apt to be closely related to concrete realities.* On the other hand, in abstract thinking and generalizing, the *nondelinquents* are stronger, and this superiority is expressed by means of the conventionally accepted intermediate ideas or symbols.

So much for differences in the constituents of intellectual capacity.

It was also found that, both as a group and in respect to each individual's scores on the different constituents of the test, the delinquents are more *erratic* in their scores on the *verbal* subtests though they were not found to show any greater variability (scatter) than the nondelinquents on the performance subtests. To put it differently, there is less consistency of abilities among the delinquents so far as the verbal aspects of intelligence are concerned.

Some Qualitative-Dynamic Aspects of Intelligence

Apart from the verbal and performance aspects of the intellectual process, there are certain *qualitative and dynamic* features which intelligence tests do not reach. These are, however, revealed by the Rorschach Test (see Chapter XIII).

They are important because they concern not only some creative processes but those which are evidently more intimately dependent upon such emotional and volitional dynamics as, for example, power of concentration, length of attention span, clarity of associative processes, concern with details, relative freedom or looseness of association of ideas, and the like.

The qualitative-dynamic aspects of intelligence, derived from the Rorschach Test, are *originality, creativity, banality, power of observation, realistic thinking, common sense, intuition, fantasy, over-verbalizing intelligence, methodical approach to problems,* and *potential capacity for objective interests.* (Ernest Schachtel and the late Anna Hartoch Schachtel, who made the analyses of the Rorschach Test protocols for this research, have defined these terms. See *Unraveling,* Chapter XVII.) It will be recognized that some of these are to some extent reflected in the Wechsler-Bellevue Test, discussed above; however, that test reveals more of the pure intellective processes, while the Rorschach Test projects outward the deeper, emotionally tinged intellectual mechanisms.

Comparison of the delinquents with the other boys shows that the two groups are quite similar in respect to originality,[4] creativity,[5] banality,[6] intuition,[7] fantasy,[8] and over-verbalizing intelligence.[9] The delinquents have *lesser* powers

[4] *Originality* "results from an unconventional way of perception, experience, or thought, and is, in its positive aspects a genuine and often productive expression of the personality; while, in its negative aspect it may lead to estrangement from the community, to a lack of common sense, to 'queerness,' and so on."

[5] *Creativity* is "the faculty of inner production regardless of quality, and may lead to artistic, theoretical, and religious inspiration as well as to the production of systems of delusions."

[6] *Banality* is "the complete or comparative inability to think in other than the most commonplace terms and concepts."

[7] *Intuition* is "the ability to penetrate quickly some or all of the factors in a given situation, experience, or task, not by conscious deductive or inductive reasoning, but by sensing the quality of the factors involved or at least one

of observation, however, and also show less potential capacity for objective interests. On the other hand—and, as the reader will realize, findings very relevant to persistency of antisocial behavior—significantly *greater* proportions of the delinquents than of the control group are *unrealistic thinkers, lack common sense, and are unmethodical in their approach to the mastery of mental problems.*

The importance of these differentiative traits is revealed through their definition:

Power of observation involves ability to note things and events accurately and at a fairly constant level, which in turn implies "a fairly accurate visual memory and a certain amount of attentive concentration." *Potential capacity for genuine objective interests* is a quality "opposed to having interests merely or predominantly for the sake of gaining prestige, earning money, having success, procuring the attention, affection, or protection of others, and so on."

Unrealistic thinking is "a manner of thinking and perceiving in which reality is unduly distorted by phantasies, wishes, fears, and anxieties."[10] *Common sense* is "the faculty of thinking and acting in the ways of the community; it may be present even if some acts of the individual run counter to accepted mores; there may be, for instance, a conflict between common sense and a phantastic search for adventure." A *methodical approach to problems* is the "systematic way in

---

aspect of their quality. Intuition, therefore, does not necessarily lead to constructive results. If it is combined with a lack of mental control or with flightiness, it may lead to an entirely distorted mental picture of a situation or to a quite inadequate solution of a problem."

8 *Fantasy* is a tendency to "the invention of something which is not taken from reality, or the combination of elements taken from reality in a way not conforming to reality."

9 *Ververbalizing intelligence* reflects "the ability to speak or write on a rather high level of fluency and variety of ideas without, however, having corresponding breadth and depth of experience, thought, and feeling."

10 It should be pointed out that this quality, although more frequent among the delinquents, exists in but small proportions of both groups of boys.

which a mental problem or some task is approached and in which the individual tries to master it."

The above analysis has shown that our delinquent group is somewhat more apt in those intellectual tasks in which the approach to meaning is by direct physical relationships with a minimum of dependence on intermediate symbols or abstract thinking. As a group and individually, also, the delinquents are more erratic in their intellectual capacities than the more consistent and steady nondelinquents.

While the two groups resemble each other in many of the more qualitative and creative expressions of intelligence (originality, intuition, fantasy, to review but a few), they differ in others which would seem to be closely associated with capacity or incapacity to make successful conventional adjustments to the demands of social life. Thus, we have seen that fewer delinquents have adequate powers of observation and fewer show a potential capacity for objective interests; and to a significantly greater extent than the control group the delinquents are unrealistic thinkers, lack common sense, and are unmethodical in their approach to problems.

Reflection upon these differences, especially the ones involving the deeper intellectual tendencies of the two groups of boys, suggests that they are the ones which are especially interwoven with deep-rooted emotional stirrings. They are, therefore, the very mental tendencies likely to be involved not only in ability to cope with ordinary school tasks, but also in the general processes of socialization and adjustment to the realistic demands of life.

In arriving at such a "conclusion," however, we must remain tentative; we must not fall into the error of the blind men and the elephant. There are no doubt many boys with characteristics similar to those of the delinquents who are not lawbreakers. Our task is to discover the patterns of factors from all areas of the investigation which, in their dynamic interplay and combined weight, are very probably causal of persistent delinquency.

CHAPTER XII

A Psychiatric Size-up of Delinquents

Psychiatrists no longer confine themselves to the diagnosis and treatment of clear and extreme mental diseases, that "craziness" which the layman observes in someone suffering from delusions, hallucinations, or intellectual daze. The mental doctor of today can be very helpful in probing into the temperament and emotional processes of ordinary or slightly ill persons to determine how such personality attributes are related to their typical attitudes and behavior tendencies.

This is especially true in relation to the size-up of boys. To the skillful and experienced psychiatrist, children often reveal their emotional stresses and strains much more readily than do adults. Through long experience in interviewing boys, the psychiatrist of this research (Dr. Bryant E. Moulton) had developed a special flair for gaining quick and sympathetic rapport with a boy.

The aim of this portion of the inquiry was to obtain as objective an estimate of the emotional make-up of the 500 delinquent and 500 nondelinquent boys as could be revealed by the psychiatrist's diagnostic art. Therefore, following the original plan of the research to avoid possible circular reasoning, the psychiatrist, in interviewing the boys, did not have access to data about them from any other portions of the inquiry.

While psychiatric classifications of traits differ, we found it useful to organize the data of the interviews under these headings:

(1) Emotional Dynamics;
(2) Appetitive-Aesthetic Tendencies;
(3) Personality Orientation;
(4) Emotional Conflicts and Their Sources;
(5) Method of Resolution of Conflicts.

Let us see how much we can learn by this way of getting at what has been going on in the emotional life of 500 delinquents and their 500 matched nondelinquents.

Emotional Dynamics

In regard to many mental mechanisms which are obviously involved in determining how a person behaves, there is a substantial difference between the delinquents and the nondelinquents.

Take, for example, *emotional adequacy*. Only half as many delinquents as of the other boys (15%:31%) were found to be "adequate" in their ability to conduct or express themselves with a fair degree of efficiency. Common experience shows how often deep-seated emotional distraction gets people into trouble.

By contrast, the delinquent group contains twice as many boys whom the psychiatrist found to be *dynamic*—forceful, energetic (28.0%:14%). This is a vital element probably related to differences in basic physiologic equipment. It conforms with the findings presented in Chapter IX, "Physique and Delinquency," about the differences in physique and "growth spurt" among the delinquents and the nondelinquents.

There are also three times as many delinquents as controls who are markedly *aggressive*. While this trait was found to exist in relatively small numbers, it is one that may well play an important role in the antisocial behavior of some of the delinquents.

Another tendency which, if not properly harnessed and canalized, not infrequently gets boys into conflict with the law is an excessive *thirst for adventure,* change, excitement, or risk. This is characteristic of a great many more delinquents than of boys who rarely get into trouble (55%:18%). Obviously, if turned into harmless or socially constructive channels, this very adventuresomeness could be a desirable emotional mechanism. We have already had evidence of this trait in the way in which the delinquents used their leisure hours (see Chapter VIII).

Then there is an excessive proportion of delinquents who usually express their emotions by *extroversion,* i.e., who habitually spring into action upon any welling up of feelings (57%: 29%). Such lads typically leap before they look, and of course they frequently leap into trouble. The further finding that far fewer delinquents than nondelinquents (18%:50%) are *emotionally stable* (display harmonious and appropriate feelings and emotional reactions) indicates a related handicap of the delinquents.

When to this faulty emotional apparatus are added two other traits that make for difficulties in interpersonal relations—*suggestibility* (60%:26%) and *stubbornness* (41%: 8%)—both of which characterize many delinquents and a great many more of them than of the law-abiding lads, the emotional handicaps of the delinquent boys assume really serious proportions.

Given the opportunities, enticements, and provocatory

incidents of street life, even a few of these dynamic emotional tendencies may well lead to maladaptation and lawbreaking; the piling up of many of them in the mental life of a boy multiplies the chances of his habitual social maladjustment.

Appetitive-Aesthetic Tendencies

Now let us examine a few other traits which (if other factors do not intervene to counterbalance them) tend to make misbehavior more attractive than law-abidingness.

Many more delinquents than nondelinquents (20%:6%) were found to have marked tendencies to *sensuality* (inclination to indulge their appetites); more also (21%:14%) to *acquisitiveness* (tendency to get hold of material things or money beyond the desire for their immediate use). Here, too, there is an excessive incidence in the lawbreaking group of traits that may easily lead to persistent conflict with legal prohibitions. In respect to *aesthetic sensibility* (inclination to the refined and artistic), on the other hand, the delinquents as a group were markedly deficient (17%:39%).

Personality Orientation

There are striking differences between the two groups of boys, also, with reference to general qualities of personality that tend to make antisocial behavior habitual.

The delinquents as a group were found to be less *conventional,* a far lower proportion of them than of the nondelinquents (25%:49%) preferring the familiar, traditional, and safer forms of self-expression. Even more striking is the proportionately low incidence among the delinquents of boys who can be characterized as *conscientious* in the sense of being scrupulous about achieving their aims (9%:54%).

To these traits, which in themselves or in combination may

lead to troublesome conduct, should be added certain other basic personality deficiencies. Far fewer of the delinquents than of the other boys were found to be *realistic,* in the sense of facing actualities (8%:23%); or *practical,* in the sense of considering the feasibility of a proposed course of action before starting off on it (19%:35%).

Finally, the delinquents as a group are not only less *critical of themselves,* being unable and unwilling to size up their own faults and liabilities as well as their virtues and abilities (29%:11%), but also more obviously *self-centered* (egocentric) and unwilling to make allowances for others (14%:2%). Such traits make it difficult to help a person to help himself, and may partially account for the rather indifferent results obtained by those who attempt to "reform" some types of offenders.

Emotional Conflicts

It is quite generally recognized, nowadays, that certain early childhood experiences are likely to leave so burned-in an impress on the deepest emotional layers as to cause the growing personality to become scarred and twisted by frequent conflicts and frustrations, or to impel readily to socially maladapted conduct tendencies. Such handicapping and conflicting emotional pulls and tugs were clearly present among no fewer than three out of every four of the delinquents and twice as frequent among them as among the nondelinquents (75%:38%).

It is impossible as yet to determine the extent to which such disturbances in the deep feeling mechanisms of the boy are hereditary or acquired. But the *sources* of tension-generating impacts of the environment were much more numerous in the lives of the delinquents than in those of the nondelinquents.

Probably most serious from the point of view of maladaptation are the conflicts arising from the emotional relations within the family circle. In every aspect of these intrafamily relations explored by the psychiatrist, substantially more difficulties were found among the group of delinquents than among the law-abiding youngsters. The emotional interplay within which most of the problems arose had to do with the *relationship of the boy to his father* (23%:5%), i.e., in respect to his belief that his father measures up to his conception of what a male should be like, and with his difficulties in making a wholesome *sexual identification* (30%:12%). "It is . . . one of the essentials in the social development of the child that the social personality of each one shall match his sex in the biological sense; that is, boys must be boys and have masculine habits, and girls must have girls' habits . . . For the child . . . the road to prestige is paved with the rewards of observing the sex-appropriate code."[1] There is much more to the complications that arise out of a conflict over this than the patent explanation of the boy's attempt to "prove his manhood" by daring deeds in violation of the law. But whether one contents himself with more obvious relationships between this conflict and a tendency to antisocial behavior or accepts the elaborate psychoanalytic analysis of the mechanisms involved, it is one of the more significant sources of maladjustment to a social or legal code.

Conflicts in extrafamily associations were not so numerous. Only 59 of the delinquents and 19 of the other boys had marked internal mental stresses and strains about their *relationship to companions*. Nor, surprisingly, were strong conflicts evident concerning sexual interests, or religion, or community responsibility, or relationships to adults other than parents. *Conflicts about the future* (educational expectations, general prospects) were likewise not frequent; evidently

[1] James H. S. Bossard, *The Sociology of Child Development* (New York: Harper & Brothers, 1948), pp. 314, 315.

the boys as a group are not future-minded or planful. Similarly, *conflicts resulting from economic circumstances*—lack of money, material surroundings—were found to be infrequent, and this despite the fact that most of these boys, delinquent and nondelinquent alike, had grown up in underprivileged neighborhoods and in homes rarely above the poverty line.

Almost twice the proportion of delinquents as of the law-abiding youngsters had marked conflicts associated with feelings of physical and/or mental inferiority (33%:18%).

Method of Resolving Conflicts

Emotional conflicts are so frequent as almost to be deemed part of the normal lot of man, especially in our neurosis-inducing culture. But the above analysis deals with instances of marked and persistent emotional stress and strain. Very significant is the question, How does a boy *typically resolve* his inner emotional struggles?

The psychiatrist found a marked difference in the mental devices resorted to by the delinquents and the nondelinquents in coping with the tensions and upheavals of emotional conflict. It was established that the delinquents, to a far greater extent than the nondelinquents (68%:31%), tend to resolve their conflicts by "acting them out" (extroversion), that is, by giving overt expression to them in feeling and/or action. As a group they generally refuse to take responsibility for their behavior, letting the pressure of feelings work itself off in direct action without inhibition; and they are little concerned with whether that behavior is criminalistic or otherwise. Nevertheless, there is also greater inconsistency in how the delinquents express their emotional tensions; for more of them than of the nondelinquents (24%:6%) alternate between outflowing behavior and damming-up of their feelings.

Among the nondelinquents, on the other hand, the usual mechanism for resolving conflicts is one of turning inward (introversion) of their emotions (42% as compared with 5% of the delinquents). In self-protection against the "slings and arrows of outrageous fortune," they develop many inhibitory mechanisms. This bottling-up of their emotional stresses and strains results in a tense overalertness to maintain their defenses.

This brief analysis of the major personality differences of the delinquents and nondelinquents has shown that, so far as *emotional dynamics* are concerned, the lawbreakers as a group function on a less efficient level and they are less stable emotionally. At the same time they are more dynamic and energetic; more aggressive, adventurous, suggestible, and stubborn. This combination is likely to result in an inability or unwillingness to abide by the law's restrictions; for such boys are much inclined to impulsive, unreflective discharge of their energy drives, thereby breaking through the bonds imposed, but not sufficiently internalized, by custom and law.

Certain *sources of motivation,* especially, can get such boys into troublesome conflicts with society's codes. It will be recalled that the delinquents are much more inclined than the other boys to immediate indulgence of their appetites and are more eager to acquire material things.

To such a system of forces, which impels toward selfish satisfaction of impulse in violation of custom and law, should be added the finding that *basic personality orientations* among the delinquents make it more difficult for them to conform to acceptable standards. As a group they are less conventional than, and not nearly so conscientious in achieving their goals as, the law-abiding boys. They are less realistic in facing situations; less practical in considering the feasibility of a contemplated course of conduct; far less critical of themselves, and correspondingly more self-centered.

Moreover, there is much more in the *background* of the delinquents which is stress producing, so that a far higher proportion of them than of the other boys display emotional tensions arising from faulty father-son or mother-son relations, or attitudes toward their brothers and sisters. Many more of the delinquents have marked conflicts arising out of faulty adjustment of their problems of sexual identification; out of poor relations with companions; out of inability to make a satisfactory compromise between ambition and reality; and out of feelings of inferiority.

Typically, the delinquents tend to resolve their mental struggles through acting out their difficulties (extroversive behavior); the nondelinquents through turning them inward (introversion).

These psychiatric findings, so obviously related to the mechanisms tending to inadequate and improper social adjustment, are in general in harmony with those revealed independently by the other avenues of our exploration. Standing alone they are highly suggestive hints, not complete explanations, of why one set of boys inclined to persistent delinquency and the other managed to get along acceptably. But when fitted into the total picture, they gain significantly in causal relevancy. They tend, for example, to confirm in many respects the findings derived from the deep-probing and more objective Rorschach Test, to which we next invite the reader's attention (Chapters XIII, XIV).

CHAPTER XIII

Character Structure and Delinquency

It is usually taken for granted that the way a person gets along in life is almost wholly dependent on his "brains," i.e., his intelligence. But probings of the mainsprings of conduct and social relations tend more and more to stress the part played by temperamental and emotional forces in the development of personality and character[1] and the channeling of conduct. Intelligence is of course a powerful instrument of adaptation; but the way a person *employs* his intellect depends a great deal on the deeper dynamics of the organism—the ebb and flow of feelings—the trends, thrusts, and tensions of emotion that pull the levers behind the scenes of character and beneath the trap door of personality.

So it becomes of the utmost importance to obtain some in-

[1] These two concepts are often related, combined, or used interchangeably in the literature, largely, we suppose, from the difficulty of analyzing traits into their personality and characterial constituents. It is clarifying if we conceive personality to be the totality of physical, temperamental, emotional and intellectual makeup of an individual. Personality is neutral, so far as character is concerned. Character is personality plus the ingredients of ethico-religious or other ideals or goals that typically guide or dictate the individual's conduct. A man may have a strong or a weak personality; a judgment of his personality would be similar regardless of his ethical views or religious convictions. A man may have a good or a bad character; the judgment as to this depends upon the extent to which his actions typically conform to some accepted ethical or religious framework within which the man is judged. However, character type is related more or less to the nature of personality structure.

sight into the subsurface forces that influence make-up and behavior tendencies.

Various techniques of deep emotional exploration—psychoanalysis, hypnosis, hypnoanalysis, narcoanalysis, and others—are useful probers of the lower depths of the mind; but they are expensive and time consuming, and their findings difficult to standardize for the purpose of comparing large groups of delinquents and nondelinquents. However, a systematic and relatively simple means is furnished by a number of "projective tests." The one we selected for application to the inquiry was the Rorschach Test.

In Chapter IX, in which are compared the bodily types of delinquents and nondelinquents, we were concerned with biologic and essentially hereditary traits. In Chapters VI, VII, and VIII we brought to the reader's attention a great variety of social forces that played upon the basic organism of the boys. In the present chapter, in which we discuss certain of the dynamic emotional moorings of personality and character as laid bare by the Rorschach Test, we may to some extent bridge the gap between the human plant and the soil that nourished or malnourished it. For the personality and characterial traits that are revealed by such a test are, in a sense, the end products or admixtures of the interplay of original endowment and repeated experiences, particularly those of the first few emotionally charged years of life.

The Rorschach Test

The Rorschach Test consists of ten symmetrical ink-blots (most of them black, some colored) which look as if they had been made by throwing drops of ink on a paper and folding in the middle, resulting in a design often reminiscent of a butterfly. Through long clinical employment of the test on various groups of persons in different countries, their significance has been found to be startling in revealing the inner mental life. It has adequately proved its general value as a prober of personality and character.

The subject's reactions to the blots are projected out of the depths of his personality without his being able successfully to disguise his inner feelings and emotional attitudes. These responses are then scored and interpreted by a skilled psychologist in respect to *apperception* (i.e., the subject's general size-up of the blots), the *quality* of his reactions, and their *content*.

In regard to apperception, responses are noted and evaluated as being to the *whole* blot, to *details*, and the like. In respect to quality, three types of basic mental responses are set down: *form, movement,* and *color*. In regard to content, the subject may, for example, recognize the form of an animal, or a human being, or an object, a landscape, some anatomical pattern or some abstract design. *Originality* and *banality* (commonplaceness) of his responses also are noted and integrated into the total personality size-up.

The subject is scored on these various aspects of his responses in accordance with established standards, and his score is tabulated to yield a Rorschach *psychogram,* which provides a panoramic view of his temperamental-emotional topography, including both surface and subsurface features. In other words, the diagnosis is not based upon any single response. It is the patterning of responses that is significant.

The Rorschach Test thus projects the deeper, often subconscious, elements of mental activity in such a way that to the expert they reveal highly significant features of structure, tensions, and dynamics of character and personality.

Before presenting the Rorschach Test results, the reader must again be reminded of two fundamental matters—first, that the delinquents and the nondelinquents had been carefully matched in respect to age, general intelligence (I.Q.),

ethnic derivation, and residence in economically and culturally poor neighborhoods; secondly, that each avenue of
exploration (family and personal history, health, physique,
intelligence, temperament, character) was pursued independently. For example, the Rorschach experts (Ernest G.
Schachtel and his wife, the late Anna Hartoch Schachtel) who
scored and interpreted the test responses knew nothing about
the findings of the other parts of the inquiry at the time they
made their own assessment.

For the sake of clarity, the test results have been organized
by the Schachtels into six general categories:

(1) Basic Attitudes Toward Authority and Society;
(2) Feelings of Insecurity, Anxiety, Inferiority, Frustration;
(3) Kindliness and Hostility;
(4) Dependence and Independence;
(5) Goals of Strivings;
(6) Some General Qualities of Personality.

Since mental processes are complexly interrelated, it is
difficult to avoid some overlapping of the traits subsumed
under each of these headings. The human mind is an organic
and dynamic entity and cannot be neatly departmentalized.
However, the above categories permit of a reasonably sound
management of the detailed materials of the test interpre-
tations.

Basic Attitudes Toward Authority and Society

In the study of delinquency it is particularly important to
compare delinquents with law-abiding boys in respect to what
their usual attitudes are regarding all forms of authority—
parental, school, and that of society in general as personified
by police officers, judges, and others. " 'The process of growing

up,' says Dr. Bernard Glueck, 'is to a very large extent taken up with the problem of adjusting oneself to the guidance that comes from one or another of the authoritative sources surrounding the child; and those who have the training of the child in hand should, while recognizing the need of guidance, be 'aware at the same time of the dangers of over-guidance and of the fact that an essential element of maturity is a relative freedom from the need of guidance.' 'A nice balance between the disposition to self-esteem and the tendency to self-abasement' is essential to mental health, and 'contact with an unintelligent exhibition of parental authority may and does hamper the individual in the attainment of this nice balance. The pathological deviations may be either in the nature of an oppressive sense of inferiority and a self-depreciating attitude in the face of one's daily problems, or an ugly, overweening haughtiness of manner which frequently deteriorates into a tyrannical bullying of one's associates or dependents. The over-reaction to an oppressive authoritativeness may also lead to a chronic state of rebellion and active antagonism to all forms of authority.' "[2]

Obviously, then, the basic attitudes toward authority are of prime importance in assessing the causal forces of persistent delinquency. The fundamental traits involved in the person's attitude toward authority as revealed by the Rorschach Test are *self-assertion, social assertion, defiance, submissiveness,* and *ambivalence to authority.*

How do the delinquent boys compare with the law-abiding ones in respect to such traits?

First, as to *self-assertion,* or the faculty of affirming one's personality, rights, demands, opinions, in a direct and open manner without exaggerated aggressiveness,[3] this trait was

[2] M. B. Sayles, *The Problem Child in School* (New York: The Commonwealth Fund, 1929), pp. 15-16.

[3] Definitions are, with some simplification, those contained in *Unraveling Juvenile Delinquency,* as prepared by Ernest and Anna Schachtel.

found to play a relevant role in the character structure of less than a tenth of the delinquents and a handful of the nondelinquents.

Social assertion, or the more *surface* quality of asserting will and ambitions with regard to the environment as opposed to the development of a genuine, spontaneous self, is a trait possessed by about half of all the delinquent boys and two in ten of the nondelinquent boys (45%:21%).

The trait of *defiance* is a reactive mechanism, a form of aggressive self-assertion in response to a feeling of deep insecurity or weakness; it is, therefore, often indiscriminate in aims or means and usually directed *against* some person or thing rather than *toward* a positive goal. This personality defect, so obviously a handicap to successful social adaptation, was found to characterize half the delinquent boys as compared with one in ten of the nondelinquents (50%:12%).

The trait of *submissiveness* may be described as indicative of a giving up of self-assertiveness in the attempt to gain a sense of security through submitting to the authority of others, especially those who are believed by the child to be stronger (originally, often, one or both parents, later the anonymous power of institutions, public opinion, conventional usage, and the like). This trait, so obviously implicated in a child's problems of adjustment to the demands and standards of adults, was found to characterize the delinquents far *less* than the nondelinquents. Only about one in four of the former were found to be markedly submissive to authority as contrasted with three times as many of the nondelinquents (27%:80%).

Ambivalence to authority describes contradictory feelings of one person in relation to another, usually the coexistence of friendly and hostile strivings of love and hatred; or, as in this research, such inconsistency of feeling toward authority as the coexistence of defiant and submissive strivings, or of assertive and dependent attitudes. A contradictory feeling toward authority is another weak crutch on which to lean for successful adaptation to the demands of the socio-legal code. Here, as in other traits already noted, the delinquents are disadvantaged, for double the proportion of them as of the other boys were found to have this trait (42%:20%).

The foregoing comparison of the basic emotional attitudes of the two sets of boys toward authority and society has revealed that the delinquents are only slightly more self-assertive than the nondelinquents but *far more socially defiant, far less submissive, and more ambivalent to authority than the nondelinquents.*

It is already clear, then, that the delinquents are as a group markedly distinguishable from law-abiding youngsters by their unwillingness or inability to tame their natural instinctual impulses to self-indulgent behavior in order to bring such drives into line with the authoritative demands of the home, the school, and the larger society.

However, we must again caution the reader not to jump to conclusions. We have seen that some of these handicapping traits exist also among appreciable numbers of boys who do not violate the law. Here, again, we have a clear illustration of the need for a *multiple-causal* analysis. Without this, the parts of the puzzle of crime causation cannot be meaningfully pieced together.

Feelings of Insecurity, Anxiety, Inferiority, and Frustration

Apart from the problem of the relationship of the individual to the sources of authority, there is another area of character development in which especially significant clues regarding the dynamic causes of maladjustment might lie. This has to do with deep stirrings of emotion of a nature that might well propel a child in directions in which he would never go were he in full conscious control of his faculties in relation to ideals and standards.

Among these emotional stirrings is a general, vague, and frequently unconscious *feeling of insecurity or anxiety*. This plays a role not only in every neurosis but often also in the activities of many "normal" persons who somehow manage to go through life with enough efficiency and satisfaction "to get by." The trait in question may also be described as a feeling of having no hold, or insufficient hold, on life in general or on any specific sphere of life that may be important to the person. This vague sense of insecurity or anxiety was found to be present in large numbers of both delinquents and nondelinquents and in quite similar proportions (89%:96%). This is one of the factors, therefore, that in itself cannot be deemed as significant in causing delinquency. It is relatively "complacent" in this regard, although it may well raise important questions of why there is so high an incidence of this crippling feeling among both groups of boys and whether this is characteristic of most children in underprivileged areas or is related to the general American culture or to the special characteristics of our age.

A closely related trait—*enhanced insecurity or anxiety*—is distinguishable by the Rorschach Test from the more general and vague emotional state just discussed. The distinction is one of degree, but the skilled Rorschach diagnostician is able to make it with dependable precision. *Enhanced insecurity or anxiety* refers to a state in which such feelings clearly play a decidedly stronger role in the personality, either quantitatively or qualitatively, than is usual in the average person, even though they may remain largely outside the ken of his awareness. Although this trait was found to exist in relatively small numbers among both groups of boys, a *lesser* proportion of the delinquents than of the controls possessed such enhanced feelings of insecurity or anxiety (18%:29%).

Another deep-seated emotional trait is the *feeling of not being wanted or loved*. Often repressed and therefore unconscious, it may nevertheless lead to an exaggerated need for affection, recognition, success, and the like. It is a belief that one is not accepted, not included, or is even rejected by others; a feeling of a lack of positive human relationship to a particular group or person. It is of special importance with regard to the sympathetic relationship to one's own family (especially the parents) in early childhood. It should be pointed out that the feeling of not being wanted or loved can coexist with, and in fact is often actually produced by, an overprotective attitude or other form of possessive parental "love." Although both parent and child may believe that a loving and affectionate relationship exists, unconsciously the child feels that he is not really wanted and loved for himself but as the property, as it were, of the parent.

This *feeling of not being wanted or loved* is generally looked upon as a powerful cause of delinquency. But, as it is found to exist in quite similar proportions among both the delinquents and their matched nondelinquents (92%:97%), it cannot play a significant causal role. Once more a highly significant question is presented as to why this feeling is so general among our boys. The fact that there is more warmth and affection between the parents and the boys in the case of of the nondelinquents (Chapter VI) does not place either set of findings in dispute. Parents may be or seem to be devoted to their children and yet, for the reasons already indicated, there may be built into the unconscious layers of the child's personality a feeling of not being wanted or loved.

The *feeling of not being taken care of,* closely related to the feeling of not being wanted or loved, arises from an absence of active interest or care and help in a situation in which the person feels entitled to such interest, especially in the child-parent relationship. As is true of so many of the emotional deposits of childhood, this feeling, once created, may outlast the situation that originally produced it. Here again, however, little difference was found between the delinquents and the nondelinquents in respect to the presence of this trait in the character structure (29%:24%).

Similarly, no significant difference emerged between the two groups of boys in respect to the *feeling of not counting,* that is, that one's own person, interests, ideas, and wishes are not acknowledged and not treated as deserving of respect and consideration for their own sake. This trait, in marked or slight degree, characterized over half of both groups of boys (59%:64%).

The *feeling of not being recognized* (the belief that one's qualities, intentions, or achievements are not sufficiently appreciated, a feeling often associated with conscious and unconscious grandiose ideas about one's self) was found to be more excessive among the delinquents than the nondelinquents (36.1%:24.5%).

The *feeling of helplessness or powerlessness* is a particularly important though often unconscious kind of sense of insecurity, the individual deeply believing he can neither change nor influence anything, especially his life course. Fewer of the delinquents than of the nondelinquents had this emotional attitude (42%:54%).

The delinquents were also found to suffer substantially less from *fear of failure or defeat,* a feeling that is a frequent consequence of anxiety, especially in persons with an over-competitive attitude. Fear of failure may concern every sphere of life—work, play, all human relations. Depending on the other constituents of the personality, it may lead either to greater effort or to inhibitions, aloofness, and recoiling from competition. Although this fear of failure or defeat is present in a surprisingly large proportion of *both* groups of boys, it is less characteristic of the delinquents (44%:63%).

Turning next to the *feeling of resentment* or frustration, envy, or dissatisfaction, this emotional attitude is far more frequent among the delinquents than among the boys within the control group (74%:51%). Persons in whom this attitude is strong are not so much concerned with the positive attempt or hope of bettering their own situation as with the desire that others should be denied the satisfactions and enjoyments which they feel is being withheld from themselves. Resentment, in other words, is different from mere envy or the wish to have what somebody else has.

The *feeling of resignation,* the belief that "it is no use," that life holds forth no promise and that things cannot be changed or improved, was found to exist among only a handful of both groups of boys and may therefore be disregarded as of little significance.

Briefly summarizing the foregoing comparisons of the basic character traits of the delinquents and nondelinquents, it will be recalled that *a significantly higher proportion of the delinquents than of the nondelinquents are characterized by feelings of not being recognized or appreciated and by feelings of resentment.* However, the delinquents as a group have an appreciably *lower* incidence of certain handicapping emotional attitudes—feelings of anxiety or insecurity, helplessness and powerlessness, fear of failure and defeat.

It should be emphasized that there is no difference between the two groups in the extent to which they feel unwanted or unloved, or not taken care of; or not taken seriously. It may well be that in the rough and tough milieu of the economic-cultural level from which the two groups stem, such feelings are common among children. While this situation is to be deplored, and ought certainly to be coped with in a responsible society, the similar incidence among delinquents and non-delinquents of such emotional attitudes makes it very unlikely that they have any close causal relationship to persistent delinquency. They may, perhaps, act as differentiative catalytic agents when other psychologic factors are brought into play.

Kindliness and Hostility

A third set of character and personality traits revolve around the basic emotional attitudes of *kindliness and hostility*. It would be expected, in the light of the fact that the delinquents are far more resentful toward authority than the boys who keep out of trouble, that they are also, in general, less cooperative, more hostile and suspicious, more on the defensive, and more destructive than the nondelinquents.

First as to *cooperativeness*, that is, ability to make surface contacts with others in common work without "mutual obstruction," the delinquents show a substantial deficiency in this characteristic as compared with the nondelinquents most of whom are cooperative (71%:97%). The importance of this trait for satisfactory social adjustment is obvious.

In respect to *kindliness and trust*, that is, the general expectation that others will be friendly, humane, trustworthy, no significant difference emerges between the delinquents and the other boys. Whether as the result of their experiences at home or in the world of the streets, this natural childhood expectancy of friendliness from those with whom they come into contact is absent in over nine-tenths of both groups (96%:93%). Here is a fact which must be pondered by parents, schoolteachers, boys' club leaders, and all who participate in molding the destinies of youth.

In overcompetitiveness, that is, in exaggeration of the competitive spirit regardless of the objective situation, no significant difference is found between delinquents and nondelinquents, the trait being largely absent, i.e., playing little role in the basic character structure of both groups (94%:92%). The popular notion that this attitude is a strong motivation of delinquent conduct receives no support.

However, with respect to the emotional attitude of *hostility*, that is, conscious or unconscious animosity toward others without normal reason for such an attitude, there is a sharp difference between the delinquents and the nondelinquents. Almost two-thirds of the delinquents have *markedly* hostile impulses toward others, as compared with a third of the nondelinquents (60%:37%). Here is a trait that might well lead to maladaptation to the normal demands of conventional living.

Closely related to feelings of hostility is an attitude of indiscriminate or excessive *suspiciousness* toward others, a feeling not warranted by the objective facts, and of which the person is usually not aware or which he interprets as mere cautiousness or realism, or as justified by supposed persecution. Here, again, there occurs a wide gap between the lawbreakers and the law-abiders. Twice the proportion of delinquents as of nondelinquents have a marked attitude of suspiciousness embedded in the personality structure (51%: 27%).

Allied to hostility and suspicion is the characteristic of *destructiveness*, an emotional dynamism obviously associated with delinquent behavior. This tendency to destroy, hurt, or, in more diluted form, to be "negativistic" or "contrary-minded," may be directed not only against others but against oneself. In the deeper emotional currents of the personality, these trends often run parallel, one being more manifest, the other suppressed. As would be expected, the delinquents have an excess of this trait, half of them possessing it in either marked or slight degree compared to a seventh of the latter (49%:15%).

In view of the finding that the delinquent boys have slightly more difficulty than the other boys in making contact with people, and are considerably more hostile, suspicious, and destructive, it might be expected that they would also have a more marked *feeling of isolation,* that is, a sense of being "alone" (often combined with a feeling of helplessness) and of not being sufficiently capable of giving and receiving affection. Sometimes this feeling is hidden beneath a perpetual surface activity of "making friends," which is motivated by an attempt to escape a sense of extreme emotional isolation. Here is another trait, however, in which the difference in incidence in the two groups is not very great (45%:36%).

Because of excessive feelings of hostility and suspicion among the delinquents, it is not surprising to discover that they are also, to a significantly greater extent than the other boys, characterized by an exaggerated *defensive attitude,* essentially unwarranted. The mechanism for expressing this attitude consists sometimes of building an emotional shell to ward off every approach and sometimes of aggressive defiance or obstinate or opinionated behavior. The delinquent group was found to contain a higher proportion of boys possessing this hard-to-penetrate defensive attitude than was found among the nondelinquents (56%:44%).

As we cast a backward glance on the two sets of boys with reference to their interpersonal relations, we must be impressed with the fact that in certain respects that are significant for social adaptation, the delinquent boys are less effectively equipped than the law-abiding ones. *As a group, the delinquents are markedly less cooperative in their relations to those with whom they are closely associated; a substantially greater proportion of them have conscious or unconscious hostile impulses; they are more suspicious of the motives of others; they are more destructive; and more of the delinquents than of the nondelinquents are armed with an exaggeratedly defensive attitude toward life.*

We continue the analysis of the Rorschach Test findings in the next chapter, where we shall deal with the three remaining sets of traits that are of crucial significance to the child in making relatively frictionless and painless adjustments to the demands of an adult world. These have to do with dependence and independence, goals of strivings, and some general qualities of personality.

CHAPTER XIV

More About Character Structure

Proceeding further with the array of deep-lying traits disclosed by the Rorschach divining rod, we see in this chapter how delinquents differ from nondelinquents in respect to the characteristics subsumed under (1) *Dependence and Independence,* (2) *Goals of Strivings,* and (3) *Some General Qualities of Personality.*

Dependence and Independence

The subsurface traits to be considered are of significance in assessing the extent to which the boys under comparison are either emotionally dependent upon others or self-reliant, independent, and secure.

The tendency to cling to others instead of standing on one's own feet reveals itself in an emotionally charged *dependent attitude* toward loved ones, employers, or others who furnish or may be expected to furnish protection. It was found to exist in substantial proportions among *both* sets of boys, a fact that may be partially due to the general economic insecurity of families residing in urban slum areas and frequently on the edge of unemployment and poverty. However, an attitude of marked dependence on others was found far less frequently among the delinquents than the nondelinquents, some seven-tenths of the former compared to almost nine-tenths of the latter being thus characterized (69%:86%).

Another personality-character trait sometimes found in this connection is an overemphasis on *meeting the expectations of others.* A sense of insecurity often leads to overconformity, whether this be to desirable socio-legal mores or to the expectations of an antisocial gang. While this feeling is absent among the great majority of the delinquents and nondelinquents, it exists to a lesser extent among the former (7%: 19%).

Conventionality in ideas and behavior is yet another of the cluster of traits involved in the general emotional pattern of dependence or independence. A far *lower* proportion of the lawbreakers than of those who conform to the legal order tend to be markedly conventional in their ideas, attitudes, and conduct. To put it differently, there are substantially more social *rebels* among the delinquents (75%:53%), as determined by other evidence than commission of crime.

There is little difference between the delinquents and the nondelinquents in respect to *spontaneity,* the genuine expression of the self in terms of experience, feeling, thought, and behavior, as opposed to artificial, conventional reactions. Some nine-tenths of both groups (92%:95%) were found to lack this ability of expressing themselves spontaneously.

Although the *feeling of being able to manage one's own life* is widely prevalent in both groups, there is a slight difference between delinquents and nondelinquents, more of the former having this feeling than of the latter (73%:64%).

Reviewing the differences between the delinquents and the nondelinquents in attitudes of dependence, we see that *the delinquents feel far less dependent on others than do the nondelinquents; are less conforming; far less conventional; and slightly more confident of their ability to handle their own problems.*

Goals of Strivings

We turn now to some typical ways in which the boys seek to obtain satisfaction of deep-seated needs—by narcissistic (or self-loving), masochistic (or self-punishing), receptive (or parasitic), and destructive-sadistic (or cruelty-inflicting) mental mechanisms.

Narcissistic trends (excessive need for admiration, status, prestige, power, superiority, and the like) are found to be *absent* in high proportions of *both* groups of boys. Nevertheless, the delinquent group reveal a substantially higher incidence of this tendency toward self-love than is found among the other boys (23%:14%).

Masochistic trends (a tendency to be dependent, accompanied by a desire to suffer), while not found excessively in the personality dynamics of either group of boys, nevertheless proved to be far less characteristic of the delinquents than of the nondelinquents (15%:37%).

Two tendencies in the quality and direction of satisfaction toward which inner strivings tend to flow are projected by the Rorschach Test: first, to receive or take in ("oral" or *receptive trends)* and, secondly, to destroy or hurt, to exercise power, to deprive *(destructive-sadistic trends)*. The first is frequently expressed in a conscious or an unconscious expectation that others (people, society in general, God) will take care of one, the person not feeling obliged to make any serious effort to help himself or to assume responsibilities. It should be pointed out that this tendency, which usually finds expression passively (the person marking time parasitically while someone else provides what he desires), may also take the active form of an inclination to greed or even to criminalistic attempts to secure desired objects without honest effort.

As might be anticipated, it was found that the delinquent group is characterized by a substantially higher incidence of receptive trends than are the nondelinquents (30%:14%).

As concerns *sadistic trends* (the tendency to destroy, to hurt), the delinquents are again found to have this trait in greater measure than the law-abiding boys (49%:16%).

It is clear, therefore, that *the law violators as a group are more narcissistic (self-loving), more orally receptive (parasitic), and more destructive-sadistic (cruel) than the boys who conform to the legal order. Correlatively, they are far less masochistic (self-punishing) than the law-abiding boys.* Here are personality and character traits that are obviously related to a tendency to antisocial behavior. Yet small numbers of the nondelinquent boys also possess these traits and there are delinquents who do not have them. It again becomes clear that no single trait or cluster of traits, even among those which are likely to be handicapping to normal social adaptation, necessarily accounts for a pattern of persistent delinquency. Evidently, there are certain combinations of traits (biological, physical, social, psychological, characterial, and so on) resulting in a pressure so strong as to tip the balance in favor of habitual antisocial responses to the problems of life.

Some General Qualities of Personality

The Rorschach Test reveals certain general personality traits which concern the manner in which the emotional drives and trends are typically expressed or discharged.

Considering first *emotional lability,* a tendency to impulsive expression of feelings, a substantial difference is found between the delinquents and the nondelinquents. Almost two and a half times as many of the former group as of the latter have this trait (44%:19%). This factor, so clearly significant in the process of adaptation, arises from certain qualities in the inner emotional-volitional equipment (including the possible role of an abnormal biologic basis), which permit drives and impulses to spill over quickly into action without the interposition of reflective thought; or allow emotional tensions to be discharged explosively, more or less regardless of consequences and beyond what is normally called for by the realistic requirements of the provoking situation.

In respect to *self-control,* or the faculty of inhibiting or redirecting the discharge of emotion, which is the opposite of emotional lability or impulsiveness, it is found, as might be expected, that the delinquents as a group are *deficient;* for they contain far fewer self-controlled boys than are found in the nondelinquent group (39%:66%).

Not only are the delinquents more labile emotionally and less self-controlled than the nondelinquents, but a far higher proportion of them than of the other boys are *vivacious,* or "lively," in their behavior tendencies. Vivacity is a basic personality trait of half the delinquents and less than a fourth of the nondelinquents (51%:23%). This, if properly canalized and directed toward legitimate goals, works no social harm and can be of great value in human relations.

Fewer of the delinquents than of the law-abiding youngsters were found to have so-called *compulsory trends* (21%:30%). This term includes both the familiar neurotic compulsions and the less dramatic, less obvious instances of a rigidity of behavior tendency which interferes with a flexible and frictionless adaptation to changing situations. This type of reaction is often an attempt to overcome unconscious anxiety. The finding that such compulsive trends exist less frequently among the delinquents than among the nondelinquents is in harmony with other findings of the research that the delinquents, as a group, are *less neurotic* than the law-abiding boys.

Still another aspect of personality dynamics revealed by the

Rorschach Test has to do with *extroversive and introversive trends,* discussed in Chapter XII in connection with the psychiatrist's size-up of the boys. These emotional outlets are generally regarded as mutually exclusive. But in "real life" they run concurrently within the personality. The difference between persons who are more apt to discharge their tensions in either emotional or motor action (extroversion) and those who are more apt to allow tensions to pile up and to live within themselves and with their mental fantasies (introversion) is, moreover, not necessarily and always a difference between the healthy and the neurotic. The trends themselves are neutral mechanisms, and either of them can be healthy, neurotic, or psychotic, depending upon degree and typicality. Nor are introversion and extroversion fixed patterns, but rather processes which, in pathologic cases, tend to become so rigid as to approach fixity. Here, again, the delinquents are different from the other boys, over half of them, compared to a third of the nondelinquents (55%:35%) being extroversive in action and/or feeling. This tendency to discharge emotion and tension in direct, unreflective action is a personality trait which, if not exercised in a favorable or harmless environment, can lead to maladaptation of a kind which the law prohibits.

These findings of the Rorschach Test, made independently of the psychiatric examination and by other experts, confirm those arrived at by the psychiatrist in his interviews with the boys.

As regards predominance of *introversive trends* (usually characterized by the tendency to pile up emotional tension, to preoccupation with the more creative mental processes, to living more within oneself, and to difficulty in expressing oneself emotionally), no significant difference emerges between delinquents and nondelinquents. Only a fourth of each group show a preponderance of introversive trends.

Reviewing these general qualities of personality, it is again apparent that *the delinquents have certain traits and emotional dynamic tendencies which make it difficult for them to adapt to society's legal code. They are considerably more impulsive and vivacious than the law-abiding boys; less self-controlled; and they tend to act out their emotional tensions.*

Mental Pathology

The description of the basic traits, goals of strivings, and conduct tendencies of the delinquents and their matched non-delinquents presented in this and the prior chapter does not show the extent to which these characteristics occur in particular combinations or specific patterns. This we must leave to a subsequent inquiry. Nevertheless, it was possible for the Rorschach analysts to size up roughly the mental patterns of each delinquent and nondelinquent in terms of a general mental diagnosis.

It is apparent that there are some differences between delinquents and nondelinquents in the extent and nature of *mental abnormality or pathology.* (These diagnoses were corroborated by independent classifications made by the staff psychiatrist. See *Unraveling Juvenile Delinquency,* p. 242, footnote 8.) A slightly higher proportion of the lawbreakers than of the law-abiding youngsters was found to have a mental abnormality of one kind or another (51%:44%). Many more delinquents than boys in the control group are described by the Rorschach analysts as "poorly adjusted, asocial, poorly adapted, or 'primitive,' " apart from their acts of delinquency (17%:6%).

On the other hand, neither definite *psychoses* (two delinquents and eight nondelinquents having disorders of the schizophrenic type) nor *disturbances of the central nervous system* (four delinquents, one nondelinquent) play a significant role in the lives of these two sets of boys.

Although it is often claimed that many delinquents are "psychopathic"[1] or show marked trends toward such a condition, only 36 (7.3%) of the 500 delinquents and 2 of the nondelinquents (0.4%) were thus characterized by the Rorschach analysts. The difference in incidence of psychopathy in the two groups is of course marked; but since it involves so few boys, psychopathy need not be emphasized in assessing the more pervasive causes of delinquency. (The telltale marks that justify an incontrovertible diagnosis of psychopathic personality, difficult to be sure of even in adulthood, may not be fully apparent in boyhood.)

Severe neuroticism was found to exist among only 3.2% of of the delinquents and 5.1% of the other boys. However, *mild neuroticism* (a condition in which the neurosis does not prevent the individual from quite efficient and not too painful a social adaptation) was found among 16% of the former and 23% of the latter. Youths with distinct neurotic trends but not classifiable in the two former categories amounted to 5% among the delinquents, 8% among the nondelinquents.

Totaling all the boys diagnosed as marked or mild neurotics or having neurotic trends, it becomes clearer that there is less neuroticism among the delinquents as a group than among the nondelinquents (25%:36%).

Thus, significant differences exist between the delinquents

[1] *Psychopathy* (or psychopathic personality) is clinically distinguishable from well-marked psychoses, on the one hand, and neuroses, on the other. The psychopath is sometimes spoken of as "less ill than the psychotic and more ill than the neurotic." The reader will agree that this is a somewhat vague and nonuniform concept. Nevertheless, the psychopath is simply distinguishable from the neurotic in being more often openly destructive and antisocial or asocial, and less amenable to therapeutic or educational efforts. The Rorschach experts used the term to designate all marked mental and emotional deviations that do not clearly belong in any one of the other diagnostic groupings.

and the nondelinquents in the nature of, but not in the extent of, mental pathology. This derives largely from the higher proportion of psychopathic and "primitve" personalities among the delinquents and more neurotics among the nondelinquents.

To summarize, while there are considerable variations in the extent to which the different characteristics revealed by the Rorschach Test exist among all the boys, *there can be not the slightest doubt that the delinquents possess in excess traits and tendencies that are likely to interfere with adequate and wholesome adjustment to the requirements of the social order.* In much greater proportion than their nondelinquent counterparts they are defiant and ambivalent toward, and/or less submissive to, authority. They are more resentful. They are far more hostile, suspicious, and destructive. The goals of their drives are to a far greater extent both oral-receptive (parasitic) and destructive-sadistic. They are definitely more impulsive and less self-controlled.

As if these trouble-brewing ingredients are not enough, the delinquents are at the same time far less cooperative and markedly less conventional in their ideas, feelings, and behavior.

Some of the traits possessed in excess by the delinquents are of a kind which, if guided into socially acceptable channels, are far from undesirable. Such characteristics as a tendency to "act out" their difficulties (extroversion), greater freedom from fear of failure and defeat, and less dependence on others, might, under proper circumstances, be assets rather than liabilities.

This fact, and the marked differences in incidence of so many of the personality-character traits of boys growing up in underprivileged areas, should strikingly convince the reader that, *while the study of environmental pressures is important, study of how different children respond to these pressures is of crucial importance. It is not alone exposure to unwholesome environmental experiences that explains delinquency, but rather what these experiences mean in terms of the shaping of personality and character and the canalizing or sublimating of primitive impulses.*

If we reflect on the differences between the two groups of boys in their basic character traits, we begin to note that they are not altogether haphazard but tend to fall into a general, meaningful personality pattern, despite the fact that there are hints here and there of subpatterns. They form themselves into a cluster of *associated energy- and emotion-expressing characteristics of the uninhibited, untamed, unreflective child.* There is little mystery about the causes of persistent maladapted, delinquent behavior when one considers the ease with which modern urban conditions supply the theater of action for boys of this nature.

But again let us give pause before we "button up" our conclusions regarding causative forces in persistent delinquency. Here, as in the other chapters dealing with the findings of this many-sided inquiry, we must not let the facts of any single avenue of exploration serve as a definitive explanation. We must synthesize each set of facts into a pattern that "makes sense" and which in turn can be clinically tested on other samples of delinquents and nondelinquents.

CHAPTER XV

Riddle of Delinquency

In the preceding chapters we have disentangled and laid bare
for the reader the separate strands of difference between the
delinquent boys and their nondelinquent counterparts.
Throughout the process the reader has been cautioned to
reserve his conclusions about "the causes of delinquency"
until the findings of all lines of the inquiry are before him and
he can reflect upon them *in unison.* For to leave the various
strands of the complex knot as they have been disentangled
would not bring him as close to the heart of the riddle of
causation as the research materials permit. In reviewing those
factors which distinguish, and often markedly so, the delinquents from the nondelinquents, we should note whether the
strands lend themselves to a reweaving into a pattern that
"makes sense" from the point of view of cause-and-effect and
therefore of therapeutic and prophylactic endeavor.

The Meaning of "Cause"

Let us first be clear as to what is meant by causation—
something that seems simple enough but that is fraught with
perplexing difficulties. Several issues have to be examined:

(a) IS THERE SUCH A THING AS CAUSE-AND-EFFECT? This may
strike the reader as a superfluous question; but there has long
been debate among philosophers and scientists as to the
meaning, and even the reality, of the very concept of cause-

and-effect. It is often urged that causal connection is only *inferential* in character rather than something that can be directly perceived by the senses. "What we perceive is *sequence* of events; and it is from their sequence that we feel justified in *inferring* their causal connection, provided certain conditions are satisfied."[1]

Along similar lines James Bryant Conant, discussing the difference between biologic phenomena and those of chemistry and physics, says: "If repeated observation shows that event A always precedes event B, we accept as a matter of common sense that A is the cause, B the effect, although we realize that there is possible a long argument as to whether some earlier event was not the 'real' cause of B, or perhaps of both A and B. A boy throws a stone through a neighbor's window. What is the cause of the broken glass? The stone, the boy, the friend who put him up to the defiant act? The important point is the sequence of events in time. Except in a moving picture run backward we do not observe in common life such a series of events as broken window, unbroken window, stone near the window, stone in boy's hand, etc. Biological phenomena are events in time not unlike the simple case just cited."[2]

While recognizing the fundamental significance to the idea of cause-and-effect of *sequence in time,* we can rationally assume, further, that if such sequence occurs consistently in a definite order from the presence of a certain combination of factors to the presence of persistent delinquency, then these "successive events not only *follow,* but *follow from* one another."[3] In other words, we can legitimately assume, for practical purposes, the existence of a system of cause-and-effect in the generally accepted sense. We can, moreover, test it by

[1] *Encyclopaedia Britannica,* 1942, Vol. 5, p. 62 (italics for "inferring" supplied).

[2] Conant, J. B., *Science and Common Sense* (New Haven: Yale University Press, 1951), p. 238

[3] *Encyclopaedia Britannica, op. cit.,* p. 62.

experiments designed to modify or eliminate the conditions that have been found to precede delinquency in one sample of cases so that we may check on whether or not the subsequent result in the new sample turns out to be delinquency or non-delinquency.

This matter of causal sequence is important, further, because it dictates that in marshaling the factors which have proved to differentiate delinquents from nondelinquents, our causal conception requires that we eliminate from consideration such factors, for example, as membership in gangs, which occurred, in the vast majority of instances among our delinquents, *after* they had become delinquent, and could not therefore have been causal in the above-described sense. It will be recalled that the onset of persistent misbehavior tendencies was at the early age of seven years or younger among 48% of our delinquents, and from eight to ten in an additional 39%, making a total of almost nine-tenths of the entire group who showed delinquent tendencies before the time when boys generally become members of organized boys' gangs. The leading authorities on the subject recognize the gang as "largely an adolescent phenomenon."[4] For example, of some 1,200 cases of gang membership studied in Chicago, only 1.5% of the boys were six-twelve years old, while 63% were classified as adolescents.[5]

Basically, then, it is important in considering causal factors in the biosocial field not to put the cart before the horse.

(b) "CAUSE" REQUIRES A TOTALITY OF CONDITIONS NECESSARY TO THE RESULT.   "As a rule a cause is complex—it consists of a number of conditions each of which is only a part of

---

[4] Thrasher, F. M. *The Gang*, (Chicago: University of Chicago Press, 1936), 2nd Rev. Ed., p. 36. "The lure of the gang is undoubtedly due in part to the fact that the gang boy is in the adolescent stage which is definitely correlated with gang phenomena. Although this period has no exact limits for any individual, it includes broadly for the boy the years from twelve to twenty-six." *Ibid.*, p. 80.

[5] *Ibid.*, p. 74.

the cause."[6] It is very doubtful whether, standing alone, any *single* factor that we have disentangled in the preceding chapters would be sufficient to account for persistent delinquency. Take, for example, the fact that twice as many delinquents as nondelinquents were found to be of the closely knit, muscular, athletically inclined (mesomorphic) type. The very fact that 30% of the *non*delinquent lads also were of this physique immediately contradicts any conclusion that *mesomorphy* inevitably "causes" persistent delinquency. Or, consider such a trait as *defiance,* which one would naturally regard as closely related to delinquent behavior tendencies. True, 50% of the delinquents had this characteristic, but 12% of the nondelinquents also had it; and the very fact that half the delinquent group did *not* display this trait further reveals the inadequacy of conclusions about causation derived from a single factor.

Thus, a single factor (or even a small group of factors) may be involved, even frequently involved, in delinquent behavior and yet each one may not of itself be of sufficient weight or potency to tip the scales among boys who remain nondelinquent. In other words, "the cause of a certain effect is that *totality* of conditions that is sufficient to produce it."[7]

(C) A VARIETY OF CAUSAL PATTERNS CAN ACCOUNT FOR A SIMILAR RESULT. The fact above noted that as many as half the delinquent group were *not* characterized by the trait of *defiance* is but one illustration of the absence among a considerable group of delinquents of characteristics which are present in some other large group of delinquents. It reveals the usually unrecognized truism that persistent delinquency can be the result of not only *one specific* combination or pattern of factors that markedly differentiate delinquents from nondelinquents, but of each of several *different* combinations. This is the concept of *"Plurality of Causes,* or the view that

6 *Encyclopaedia Britannica, op. cit.,* p. 63.
7 *Encyclopaedia Britannica, op. cit.,* p. 63.

the same kind of effect may in different instances be produced by different kinds of causes."[8] Just as the fact of a boy's death, although always the *same terminal event,* may nonetheless be the result of *various preceding sequences* of conditions, so the terminal event of persistent delinquency may have in its causal background a variety of different sequences leading to the same ultimate result. For we are dealing with a complex aggregation of many internal and external conditions which are associated with socially maladjusted, unlawful behavior, and not all of them may always be *indispensable* to the result.

In criminal conduct, as in most other forms of human expression, every person has his individual resistance point or breaking point. It is difficult for all members of any society at any one time to conform to the requirements and prohibitions of socially acceptable conduct, because this involves a subordination of the natural impulses of sex expression, aggression, and the like, to those conduct norms which the law has declared necessary to the general welfare. But most persons are able (through various combinations of numerous factors of native endowment and elaborate conditioning in home, school, and society) to meet the ordinary requirements of the major legal standards of the age and place wherein they live. If a boy persists in delinquency, it means that his power of resistance to natural impulse, or his desire to obey sociolegal mandates, has been overbalanced by the strength of the other circumstances that incline to antisocial behavior.

These circumstances can consist of any combination of factors, so long as they add up sufficiently to that "totality of conditions" necessary to overbalance inhibitions. That is why there can be a "plurality of causes" in delinquency. The present *general,* or mass, comparison of data analyzed in the preceding chapters does not involve any differentiation of a possible *variety* of causal patterns or syndromes each of which

[8] *Ibid.*

is sufficient to turn the scales in favor of persistent antisocial maladjustment. In this book the delinquents are treated as a single group. In subsequent volumes we plan to describe several different patterns of factors each of which, probably, would be of sufficient weight to incline boys to persistent delinquency.

(d) "CAUSE-AND-EFFECT" IN THE SENSE OF HIGH PROBABILITY OF PERSISTENT DELINQUENCY. Closely related to the preceding concept is the matter of *probability*. Even the physical sciences, nowadays, state their generalizations in terms not of absolute inevitability but only of high probability. The statistical method of comparing delinquents, as a group, with nondelinquents, as a group, is not designed to bring out any point-to-point causal sequence that will always hold good for each and every case. It is rather intended to disclose whether or not an entire group having a certain cluster of factors in its make-up and background will much more probably turn out to be delinquent than a group of boys not so loaded down; or, to put it differently, whether the "typical," or "average," delinquent is likely to be the result of such a concatination of factors.

In other words, we are concerned with the discovery of a *general relationship between certain preceding factors and a tendency to a specific subsequent course of conduct.* Having discovered even such a general relationship, we have at hand some of the crucial information necessary as a guide to experimental programs of therapy and prevention, for we can now attack, singly or in groups, those factors which have been found to contribute most frequently and most heavily to the tendency in question.

Riddle of Delinquency

How, then, can we view the findings of marked differences between the persistently delinquent boys and the nondelinquent boys in terms of causation?

By making the reasonable inference that where so many factors preceding the fact of persistency in delinquent behavior are found in excess among the boys who became delinquents, there is a high probability of a functional, causal relationship between those factors and a tendency to persistent antisocial behavior even though there can as yet be no tracing of the "specific links in the chain of causation" in the way that clinicians attempt case by case. In other words, where a considerable number of factors that "make sense," from the point of view of common experience, are found to characterize delinquents far more than nondelinquents, it becomes highly probable that we are dealing with some sort of causal *connection* between the factors and the behavior, rather than with casual or accidental *coincidence* between them.

This of course does not mean that every boy possessing one or even several of these highly differentiative traits must inevitably become delinquent. Indeed, as we know from the fact that many nondelinquents possess some of these distinguishing traits, even a group of such factors derived from any single *area* of the inquiry is not, standing alone, too likely to result in delinquent behavior in a large proportion of instances.

Of course, in this complicated matter of what causes human beings to act persistently in one way or the other, we must also take into account the possibility that the factors we have been able to study may, in the long run, not be "ultimately causal." It will be recalled from the illustration of the boy and the broken window that "there is possible a long argument as to whether some earlier event was not the 'real' cause." As Karl Pearson puts it, "if we take an actually existing group of perceptions, say the particular ash tree in my garden, the cause of its growth might be widened out into a description of the various past stages of the universe. . . Practically, science has to content itself with tracing one . . . range of causes at a time, and this not for a special and individual object like the ash tree in my garden, but for ash trees or even trees in general."[9] Yet for many practical purposes of understanding delinquency and planning therapy and prophylaxis, it is enough to take hold of the chain of events at a "stage in a routine of experience" that we have been able to study in this research.

It may be that some day variations in the way people conduct themselves will be explainable in the more ultimate terms of differences in endocrine gland structure and function, or of microscopic physico-chemical reactions. However, we can in the meantime reasonably speak of cause-and-effect when we disentangle even the cruder forces at play in inclining persons to one course of behavior or another, just as chemistry and physics opened the doors to the solution of many problems of nature even before the dawn of nuclear science. The question is, whether such an explanation in the field of our concern brings us closer to an understanding of delinquency and therefore to its control. If it does, then, even though we are dealing with forces which may someday be reduced to more subtle constituents, we have made a stride forward in the understanding and possible management of delinquent behavior.

Untying the Knot of Delinquency

Before reweaving the separate strands of differentiation between delinquents and nondelinquents into a meaningful causal pattern, we must first lay aside all those factors which were found to exist to *similar* extent among both delinquents and nondelinquents. These elements of the dynamic system of forces may be regarded as neutral and as probably playing little or no role in the total situation.[10] Some of these "complacent" factors, as well as those in which there was but slight difference between the two groups of boys, are surprising. For

9 Pearson, *The Grammar of Science* (Everyman's Library 1949), p. 114.

10 The reader interested in these "complacent" factors will find them presented in *Unraveling Juvenile Delinquency*, pp. 272-273.

instance, there exists a marked feeling of not being wanted or loved among 84% of the delinquent boys and 88% of the nondelinquents! Such a finding shows how widespread among children in underprivileged areas is the deep-seated sense of insufficient love. Whether this is a phenomenon of the general culture we are not in a position to say; but it is so prevalent that, like residence in an underprivileged area, it largely affects both sides of the delinquency-nondelinquency equation. Therefore, unless it operates specially when combined with other factors in respect to which the delinquents do markedly differ from the nondelinquents, it must be taken to be causally neutral.

If we therefore lay aside such factors as are common (or nearly so) to both sets of boys, we are left with a large array of factors and conditions which exist in considerably different degree among the delinquents and the nondelinquents.

We have seen that such earmarks were disclosed within each area of the inquiry in which the make-up and background of the two groups of boys were explored. But before we review them we should remind the reader that in examining the strands in the tapestry of delinquency it is difficult to differentiate the warp of hereditary (genetic) factors from the woof of environmental (cultural) factors. At the present stage of human genetics it is too early to arrive at solid conclusions regarding the relative degrees of participation of various specific biologic and social factors in human behavior, whether delinquent or nondelinquent. The mechanisms of human heredity are as yet far from clear, especially where temperamental-emotional abnormalities are involved. Birth injuries or anomalies of embryologic development may be confused with truly inherited conditions; social "inheritance" may be mistaken for biologic.

Just the same, our data do permit of a rough division. On the one hand, we have the factors that are closer to the genetic than to the environmental end of the biosocial scale; on the other, we can quite clearly detect those which are nearer to the "conditioned" or acquired sociocultural end of the spectrum.

The data probably nearest to genetic roots are those dealing with bodily form (physique). Here, the reader will recall that the most striking finding is the high incidence in the delinquent group of *mesomorphic* (muscular, solid) dominance in the bodily structure. Further, the delinquents as a group have less disharmony in physique, a condition which may well facilitate easy-flowing, energetic behavior. To this should be added the finding of the delayed growth spurt among delinquents (occurring early in puberty), which may also have important implications for energetic behavior tendencies; it may be the result of the piling up of physiologic tensions (perhaps involving some early atypical functioning of the endocrine glands) culminating in the rapid discharge of an accumulated growth tendency; and this, in turn, may account in some measure for difficulties of adaptation. These possibilities are fortified by findings from other parts of the inquiry indicating differences in energy tendencies and emotional output between the delinquents and the nondelinquents.

Turning now to their health, standard medical examination revealed little difference between the two groups. Both are in equally good health. However, a considerably higher proportion of the delinquents had been bedwetters, and very "restless" in their earliest years; but a significantly *lower* proportion of the delinquents was found to have evidences of neurologic abnormalities.

Reviewing next the basic dynamics of personality and character as revealed by the Rorschach Test (which projects essentially subconscious materials), we found the delinquents to be considerably more extroversive in their trends of action, more vivacious, more emotionally labile or impulsive, more destructive and sadistic, and, in general, more aggressive and adventure-seeking, than the nondelinquents. Accompanying these outflowing temperamental-emotional tendencies is a lesser self-control among the delinquents.

In respect to a cluster of traits which may be called *emotional attitudes* in contrast to dynamisms, we found an excess among the delinquents of factors which would tend to make "walking the strait and narrow path" very difficult—hostility, defiance, resentfulness, suspiciousness, social assertiveness, and a feeling of not being appreciated.

To these handicapping traits should be added an excess among the delinquents of oral-receptive (parasitic) trends (unconsciously motivated by a desire to be looked after without effort); narcissistic desires (reflecting a strong thirst for power and status); unconventionality, noncooperativeness, disinclination to meet the expectations of others, nondependence upon others, and—especially important in the problem of delinquency—nonsubmissiveness, or ambivalence, to authority.

But it will be recalled that this faulty apparatus for legitimate social adaptation was supplemented by still other handicaps. The psychiatric examination disclosed the delinquents as a group to be more stubborn, egocentric, less critical of themselves, and more sensual than the nondelinquents. They are also far less conscientious, less practical and realistic, less aesthetic, less "adequate" in general. They are, further, much more conflict-ridden than the nondelinquents, these emotional stresses arising from a wide variety of situations—feelings of inferiority, inadequate sexual identification, unsatisfying relationship to father, to mother, and to companions.

Fitting into what we have already seen regarding energy propulsions, the delinquents largely resolve their conflicts by *acting them out* (extroversion of action or feeling, usually the former) rather than keeping them more or less bottled up as many nondelinquents do.

The instruments of adaptive or maladaptive behavior are

not only physical, physiologic, temperamental, and emotional, but also intellectual; so this strand, too, had to be unraveled from the Gordian knot of cause-and-effect. Remembering that the two groups of boys were matched at the outset in respect to general intelligence (I.Q.), the delinquents were nevertheless found to differ from the other boys in that fewer of them had the capacity to approach problems methodically, a trait which bears on the power to reflect upon contemplated behavior and assess its consequences. The delinquents as a group were found to have less verbal ability, although attaining a somewhat better score than the other boys on some performance tests. In general, the delinquents tend to express themselves intellectually in a direct, concrete manner rather than through use of intermediate symbols or abstractions. This tendency toward direct, concrete ways of mental expression as opposed to verbalistic or symbolic may be related to the general picture of the delinquents as more simply organized physically (more harmonious in physique).

There are certain forms of maladaptive behavior, in and out of school, which cannot be definitely included among the causal pressures to delinquency because they are largely *consequences* rather than *causes;* but they are relevant here because they reflect the operation of dynamisms that are frequently also involved in delinquency. These forces and resultant character traits, their roots sunk deep in early childhood, make themselves evident in such areas as school retardation, school misbehavior, general maladapted or antisocial tendencies, harmful use of leisure, and choice of undesirable companions.

Although school retardation, for example, cannot be regarded as a factor causal of delinquency (in the sense described above), it does reflect intellectual and temperamental difficulties and variations in early environment and training akin to those which are involved in making for delinquency. Thus, it will be recalled that far more of the delinquents than of the nondelinquents vehemently disliked school and far fewer had any desire for education beyond grammar school; that the scholarship of the former was much poorer than that of the latter. In excessive proportions, the delinquents revealed themselves as misfits in the school situation, were less interested in academic tasks, less attentive, more often tardy, less reliable, more careless, lazier, more restless, less truthful, and more inclined to attention-seeking behavior.

Here, again, there are strands of the delinquent pattern in evidences of restless energy with accompanying difficulties in social adaptation at the school level, and in conformance to a regime of rules and discipline involving distasteful intellectual tasks, persistency of effort, and control of impulse.

But it is in school misbehavior that we get the more striking reflection of those forces and trends more directly implicated in delinquency. Misconduct in school characterized almost all the delinquents, compared with less than a fifth of the control group. The average age of first school misconduct was nine and a half among the delinquents, or fully three years earlier than among the relatively few nondelinquents who misconducted themselves.

Frequent truancy, characteristic of so large a proportion of delinquents, clearly shows a persistent attempt to escape from the restraints of a controlled social situation. But other forms of misconduct in which the delinquents greatly exceed the nondelinquents also reflect temperamental-emotional difficulties of adaptation—disobedience, disorderliness, stubbornness, sullenness, impertinence, defiance, impudence. In smaller proportions, but consistently in much larger measure than among the nondelinquents, the antisocial boys were found to be quarrelsome, cruel, domineering, and inclined to destruction of school materials.

Whether some of these forms of misbehavior in school, which represents the first discipline-imposing institution of organized society outside the home, are largely the result of deep-rooted somato-temperamental traits or are essentially "conditioned," or are "reactive mechanisms," they all fit consistently into the temperamental-emotional segment of the general pattern that has gradually emerged as distinguishing delinquents from nondelinquents.

The same may be said of the out-of-school forms of misconduct in which, again, the delinquents by far exceeded the misdeeds of the nondelinquents. Thus, to a much greater extent than the control group, the delinquents early acquired the habits of stealing rides, sneaking into theaters without paying, "hopping" trucks, committing acts of destructive mischief, setting fires, running away from home, bunking out, and keeping late hours. Also in marked excess over the others, the delinquents gambled, begged, and began to smoke or drink at a very early age. In all this there is further evidence of a driving, uninhibited energy propulsion and thirst for adventure on the part of the delinquents.

These characteristics are also reflected in the ways in which the delinquents typically use their leisure. Less than half as many of the delinquents as of the nonoffenders spent some of their spare time at home, far more of them preferring to play in distant neighborhoods, to hang around street corners, vacant lots, waterfronts, railroad yards, poolrooms; and they gravitated toward the more exciting and unsupervised street trades in after-school jobs. They also sought vicarious adventure through movies more extensively than did the nondelinquents.

Correlatively, the delinquents were far less inclined than the other boys to supervised recreational activities and far less willing to spend any of their leisure hours in the circumscribed areas of playgrounds. (This dislike of controlled environments, even for brief periods, may also partially explain the fact that a far higher proportion of the delinquents than of the nondelinquents neglected their church duties.)

In their choice of companions, also, the delinquents differed markedly from the other boys, almost all of them (in contrast to very few of the nondelinquents) preferring to chum with other delinquents and over half of them (compared with less than 1% of the other boys) having become members of gangs.

In far greater measure than the control group, the companions of the delinquents were older boys—possibly indicating a search for temperamentally congenial "ego-ideals" to replace their own fathers to whom they were not as a rule closely attached and whom they did not admire.

Thus, in their recreational activities and companionships, the delinquents give further evidence of an inordinate craving for adventure and for opportunities to express restless, aggressive energy tendencies, with the added need of supportive companionship in such activities.

We must not, however, make the mistake of attributing the tendency to persistent delinquency entirely to temperamental or emotional propulsions. There are thousands upon thousands of boys with quite similar make-up who manage to live within the restraints of the legal code. Obviously, there is more to the causal complex than what has already been considered. Perhaps the natural tendencies of the delinquents were facilitated by their home situation and their general cultural background. A review of such factors should shed further light on the reasons for their difficulties in social adaptation.

Character is the result not only of natural equipment but also of training. Means of "sublimation" or of wholesome, or at least of harmless, channeling of energy, as well as "knowledge of right and wrong," are part of the apparatus through which character is expressed. However, a boy does not function in a vacuum, but in a cultural milieu ranging from the intimate, emotion-laden atmosphere of the home to that of the school, the neighborhood, and the general society. The tendencies that nature may implant are both morally and legally neutral. It is the existence of "thou shalt nots" and laws that colors their expression as antisocial, delinquent, or criminal.

For a child to adapt acceptably to the demands and prohibitions of any specific social organization requires certain physical, temperamental, and intellectual capacities, dependent upon the particular values protected by the culture of that society through religion, law, and custom. But modern culture, especially in underprivileged urban centers, is both highly complex and ill-defined because of conflicting values. The demands made upon the growing boy by every vehicle of today's culture are numerous, involved, often subtle, and not infrequently inconsistent. This is true of the home, the school, the neighborhood, and the general, all-pervasive culture of the times. The child is told that he must be honest, non-aggressive, self-controlled; but on every hand he runs into vivid contradictory attitudes, values, and behavior in an environment that in large measure rewards selfishness, aggression, a predatory attitude, and success by any means. It does not require the wisdom of a Seneca to convince the child, early in life, that "successful and fortunate crime is called virtue."

The demands made on the growing boy, especially in the underprivileged urban area, require a great deal of adaptive power, self-control, self-management, the ability to choose among alternative values and to postpone immediate satisfactions for future ones—all this in a cultural milieu in which fixed points and agreed-upon values, or even ideals, are increasingly difficult to discern and to hold to. This means that during the earliest years, when the hard but crucially important task of "internalization" of ideals and symbols of authority is in process, desirable attitudes and behavior standards are

not sharply enough defined, or are inconsistent, leaving a confused residue in the delicate structure of personality and
character.

While responses to the complex modern culture differ with
the varying constitution and temperament of each person
subjected to it, the basic desires of the growing child, especially
as he emerges into adolescence, are similar and imperative. .
Clinical experience has shown that among these are an assured
feeling of security and affectional warmth from parents and
companions; a striving for happiness; a desire to be free from
restraint; a thirst for new experience and for the satisfaction
of curiosity.

It is in this connection that the home climate becomes of
prime importance.

How did the household conditions and parent-child relationships of the delinquents and the nondelinquents tend to
facilitate or hinder the process of "internalization of authority," the taming and sublimation of natural instinctual drives,
and the definition of standards of good and bad?

To answer this crucial question requires, first, a review of
the findings concerning the early background of the parents
of the boys; for the parents are not only the products of the
biologic and cultural systems in which they were born and
reared, but in turn the transmitters to their children of their
own biosocial heritage.

It will be recalled that we found the biosocial legacy of the
parents of the delinquents to be consistently poorer than that
of the nondelinquents. This was evident in a greater incidence
of emotional disturbance, mental retardation, alcoholism, and
criminalism among the families from which the mothers and
fathers of the delinquents stemmed. Thus, to the extent that
the parents communicated the standards, ideals, and behavior
patterns of their own rearing to their sons, the social and
perhaps partially also the biologic heritage of the delinquents
was distinctly poorer than that of the nondelinquents.

This finding should again remind us of the fact, so frequently emphasized in this book, that no single factor or even set of factors at any level can satisfactorily explain delinquency; for, although it is true, for example, that the delinquents were generally more mesomorphic (muscular, well-knit, energetic), and while it may be true that an enhanced tendency to direct and marked energy expression is related to this mesomorphic physique pattern, the entire group of powerful influences distinguishing the background and behavior of the parents of the delinquents as compared with those of the nondelinquents is also involved in the final determination of the path that such energy expression would tend to take.

This point is brought into bold relief when we recall that not only were the grandparents (and other relatives of that generation) of the delinquents more generally handicapped, but a higher proportion of the *parents* of the delinquents than of the nondelinquents suffered from serious physical ailments, were mentally retarded, emotionally disturbed, alcoholic; and, most significant, many more of them had a history of delinquency or criminalism.

Correlatively, there has been less of an effort among the parents of the delinquents to set up decent standards of conduct for the family; they have shown less ambition to improve their status; they have done less planning for the future; and they certainly have been less self-respecting.

But these are not the only ways in which the family background of the delinquent youngsters was less adequate to their proper rearing than that of the nondelinquents. There are other aspects of family life in which the delinquents were more deprived, often markedly so: a somewhat higher proportion of their parents than those of the nondelinquents faced their marital responsibilities without preparation; a far higher proportion of their marriages turned out to be unhappy; more of the homes of the delinquents than of the nondelinquents were broken by desertion, separation, divorce, or death of one or both parents, a large number of such breaches occurring during the early childhood of the boys; many more delinquents than nondelinquents had step- or foster parents; and more of them were shunted about from one household to another during their most formative years.

As for the economic status of the two groups of families, despite the fact that the boys were matched at the outset on the basis of residence in economically underprivileged areas, both sporadic and chronic dependence have been markedly more prevalent among the families of the delinquents than among the others. This typical bogging down in the "lower depths" is at least partly attributable to the far poorer work habits of the fathers but also to less planful management of the family income.

It is, however, within the family emotional climate that the most deep-rooted and persistent character and personality traits and distortions of the growing child are developed; and here again the delinquents come off much worse than the other boys.

In interpersonal family relationships we found an exceedingly marked difference between the two groups: a much higher proportion of the families of the delinquents lacked harmony and unity. Family disorganization, with its attendant lack of warmth and respect for the integrity of each member, can have serious consequences for the growing child. It may prevent the development both of an adequate sense of responsibility and of an effective mechanism for the inhibition of conduct that might disgrace the family name. Since the family is the first and foremost vehicle for the transmission of the values of a culture to the young child, lack of family unity may leave him without ethical moorings or convey to him a confused and inconsistent cultural pattern.

Apart from the lesser cohesiveness of the families in which the delinquents were reared, many more of the fathers, mothers, brothers and sisters of the delinquent group are indifferent or frankly hostile to the boys. A far lower proportion of the delinquents than of the other boys are warmly attached to their parents. Considerably more feel that their parents have not been concerned about their welfare. Twice as many of them as of the other boys do not look upon their fathers as acceptable patterns for emulation.

The greater inadequacy of the parents of the delinquents is reflected not only in all the respects already noted but in the vital matter of disciplinary practices. In far higher measure than was true of the parents of the nondelinquents, the fathers and mothers of the delinquents resorted to confusing extremes of laxity and harshness, instead of applying reasoned and just disciplinary practices.

So, also, the delinquents' parents were far more careless in their supervision of the children, this often amounting to downright neglect.

In the light of the obvious inferiority of the families of the delinquents as sources of sound personality development and character formation, it is not surprising that the boys were never adequately tamed or socialized, and that they developed persistent antisocial inclinations, even apart from the fundamental somatic and temperamental differences between them and the nondelinquents.

The Knot of Delinquency Retied

We have seen that we cannot attribute the end product of persistent delinquency exclusively to any one set of factors derived from the various levels of our exploration. The foregoing summation of the major dissimilarities between the two groups of boys indicates, rather, that the separate findings, independently gathered and compared, tend to integrate into an organic dynamic pattern (or several subpatterns) of causation neither exclusively biologic nor exclusively sociocultural, but evidently deriving from an interplay of somatic, temperamental, intellectual, and sociocultural conditions.

Such a point of view makes sense. Otherwise we are left with serious gaps in the pattern.

If, for example, we resort to an explanation exclusively in terms of somatic constitution, we leave unexplained why most boys of mesomorphic physique do not commit crimes; and we do not bridge the gap between bodily structure and conduct. Much falls between somatic constitution and behavior.

If, on the other hand, we limit our explanation to sociocultural influences, we are overlooking the obvious fact that such forces are selective; conditions do not equally affect all persons subjected to them. We have seen that our boys did not all select the same elements in the general environment, or the same types of companions, recreations, and the like. Even in underprivileged areas, most boys do *not* develop into persistent delinquents.

Finally, if we limit our explanation to the emotional distortions and unsound character development that result from unwholesome parent-child relations, we fail to account for the fact that many nondelinquents show some traits usually deemed unfavorable to sound personality-character development, such as feelings of not being wanted or not being taken care of. We are without an explanation, too, of the fact that many boys who live under conditions in which there is a dearth of parental warmth and understanding nevertheless remain nondelinquents. We cannot reasonably account for the fact that not a few boys, under conditions unfavorable to the development of a wholesome "superego," or conscience nevertheless manage *not* to become delinquents although many of them may become neurotics.

If, however, we take into account the *dynamic interplay of the differentiative factors from all these various levels and channels of influence, a rough causal explanation takes shape* which tends to accommodate these puzzling divergencies, at least so far as the great mass of the delinquents is concerned. As a *group,* our delinquents (residents in underprivileged urban areas) are distinguishable from the nondelinquents by the following chief traits and characteristics:

Physically, in being essentially mesomorphic in constitution (i.e., solid, closely knit, muscular); *temperamentally,* in being restlessly energetic, impulsive, extroverted, aggressive, destructive (often sadistic)—traits which may be more or less related to both their bodily structure and their erratic growth pattern with its physiologic correlates or consequences; *in attitude,* in being hostile, defiant, resentful suspicious, stubborn, socially assertive, adventurous, unconventional, nonsubmissive (or ambivalent) to authority; *intellectually,* in tending to direct and concrete rather than symbolic, abstract intellectual expression and in being less methodical in their approach to problems; *socioculturally,* in having been reared to a far greater extent than the nondelinquents in homes of little understanding, affection, stability, or moral fiber, by parents usually unfit to be effective guides and protectors or desirable symbols for emulation; and under conditions unfavorable to the building of a well-balanced and socially adequate character and conscience (superego).

It is particularly in the exciting, stimulating, but little controlled, and culturally inconsistent environment of the urban underprivileged area that such boys readily tend to give expression to their untamed impulses and their self-centered desires by "kicking over the traces" of conventionally dictated behavior. These tendencies are apparently anchored deeply in body and mind and essentially derive from malformations of personality and character during the first few years of life.

It will be seen that all the foregoing conditions are of a kind that in all probability *preceded* the evolution of delinquent careers; and in the sense of *sequence of events in time* may legitimately be regarded as causally connected.

It should be borne in mind that the above synthesis of causal influence derives from a *general* comparison of persistent delinquents with nondelinquents. There are doubtless small groups of offenders who would show fundamental variations from this general pattern. For example, there are instances in which the delinquents are of the thin, tallish, fragile (ectomorphic) body type rather than well knit and muscular (mesomorphic). There are delinquents who are introverted and psychoneurotic rather than outgoing and energetic. There are also *non*delinquents who have been reared in immoral and criminalistic homes. All such exceptional subtypes deserve further study, though small in number compared to the core type delineated in this book. Their more intensive consideration may well bring about some modifications in our basic analysis and synthesis. (We are at present engaged in such detailed analyses of atypical groups of delinquents.)

Meanwhile, we can say with assurance that *the high probability of delinquency is dependent upon the operation of the factors noted in the above summary from all or most of the areas thus far explored.* Taken in the mass, if boys in underprivileged urban areas have in their make-up and early background a substantial number of the factors we have found markedly to differentiate delinquents from nondelinquents, they are very likely to turn out to be delinquent. In this general sense, then, a causal relationship has been established. Various subpatterns of factors, each sufficient to be causal of persistent delinquency, remain to be analyzed out of this general complex of factors.

Certain clinicians insist that by such a method "real" causes cannot be discovered. They couple this with the dogma that "no two people are alike" and that therefore each case must be "individualized." But if it be true that in all relevant respects no two delinquents are alike, then a science of behavior is utterly impossible; each individual is a unique organism and the causes that make him delinquent are unique to him. While it is true that in certain as yet unmeasurable characteristics each individual is unique, it is also true that in a great many traits and attributes delinquents tend to resemble each other and to differ from nondelinquents. It is in this area of knowledge that we must explore causation, not in the *terra incognita* of the unique, where even the trained clinician must be ignorant. Only God can "individualize" completely. The clinician who claims that the statistical method is of no value in arriving at causal insights and that only he can determine cause-and-effect which differs in each individual case is assuming the role of the Deity. The determination of the characteristics that distinguish delinquents as a group from those which distinguish nondelinquents, is a giant stride in the study of causation that should be of great help to the clinician who has to deal with the individual case. For not only does it furnish information that can be refined in a later, more intensive series of researches, but it gives the clinician the framework within which he can orient the individual case instead of depending on that uniqueness of each child which he is in no position to assess or evaluate. Better the *network* of distinguishing traits of delinquents as a whole than the *guesswork* of causation of each unique delinquent!

What, then, can be done in the way of reducing the development of delinquent careers once this network of factors has been identified as probably causal in a large majority of cases?

Some directions toward achievement of so desirable a goal are discussed in the final chapter.

CHAPTER XVI

Paths to Prevention

A fundamental value of the research on which this book is based is the fact that certain *specific* traits and characteristics in the background, constitution, and early experiences of the boys involved have been shown markedly to differentiate delinquents as a group from nondelinquents, in depressed urban areas. Assuming such differentia to be quite typical of a general situation in such regions (and their nature and internal consistency render this probable), we have a considerable array of suggestive clues to action designed to ameliorate criminogenic conditions. We have at least a partial basis for designing preventive programs which will be pointedly directed to the things that count most, instead of haphazardly relying upon some favorite "cause," "cure," or "preventive," or galloping in all directions at once in the vain expectation of arriving at a desirable goal. Programs of delinquency prevention that are buttoned into the specific needs and conditions suggested by sound research are not likely to be wasteful, because they deal with what has been found to be *probably relevant*.

Some of the clues brought out by our investigation have been discerned in other researches;[1] but there has previously

[1] Without exhausting the notable contributions to the study of the causation of delinquency, one must mention the books of Healy and Bronner, especially *New Light on Delinquency and its Treatment*, (New Haven: Yale University Press, 1936), and Healy's classic *The Individual Delinquent* (Boston: Little, Brown & Co, 1915); Burt, C. L., *The Young Delinquent* (New York:

been no systematic comparison of a sufficiently large, carefully defined sample of persistent delinquents matched with a large, carefully defined group of nondelinquents, and compared in respect to so many verified factors in so many areas. But even this study requires a great deal more supplementation to get at deeper meanings through detailed intercorrelations of the findings in each area of the research. We are at work on that project. In the meantime there are enough specific clues for action to enable communities to begin on a program of reorientation of preventive efforts with the aim of more pointed and relevant attacks on crucial factors.

The specific factors that distinguish persistent delinquents from nondelinquents have been found to be numerous. The precise, detailed manner of their interplay in raising the tendency to antisocial behavior from a possibility inherent in all to a very high probability cannot be determined without a great deal more investigation and analysis. The tracing of intimate connections of "mental mechanisms"[2] is rather the task of the clinician dealing therapeutically with the individual than that of the planner of general prophylactic programs based on mass phenomena. The two methods complement each other in shedding light on the causal process, but the clinical method of intensive study of the individual and the drawing of judgments about causal interplay is not indispensable to either the study of causation or the designing

Appleton-Century-Crofts, 1933); Shaw, C., especially *Delinquency Areas* (Chicago: University of Chicago Press, 1929); Lindner, R., *Rebel Without a Cause* (New York: Grune & Stratton, 1945); Slawson, J., *The Delinquent Boy* (Boston: Badger, 1926). See Cabot, P. S. de Q., *Juvenile Delinquency, A Critical Annotated Bibliography* (New York: H. W. Wilson, 1946), for other studies.

[2] See Healy, W., *The Individual Delinquent, op. cit., Mental Conflicts and Misconduct* (Boston: Little, Brown & Co., 1917); Alexander, F., and Healy, W., *Roots of Crime: Psychoanalytic Studies* (New York: A. Knopf, 1935); Lindner, *Rebel Without a Cause, op. cit.*, Karpman, B., *The Individual Criminal: Studies in the Psychogenetics of Crime,* (Washington: Nervous and Mental Disease Publishing Co., 1935); Powers, E., and Witmer, H., *An Experiment in the Prevention of Delinquency,* (New York: Columbia University Press, 1951).

of efficient programs of prevention. Indeed, the method of intercorrelational study of delinquents and nondelinquents en masse can illumine the clinical technique in helping the psychiatrist, psychologist, and social investigator to determine which among numerous factors emerging from examination of the individual child and his background are probably *relevant*.

The fact that comparison of the two closely matched sets of boys discloses that each of numerous factors unquestionably differentiates large groups of persistent delinquents from nondelinquents in a way that cannot be attributable to mere chance, and the further fact that they evidently lead to a very high potential of antisocial behavior, furnish specific pathways to preventive measures.

Need for a Realistic Approach

Before we take the reader along these pathways, let us not forget that we must approach the problem of delinquency prevention with a realistic attitude. There are no "pink pills" that will "cure" delinquency; nor is there a general prophylactic agent that will prevent it in the sense that the stamping out of the mosquito-breeding swamps will prevent malaria. If the reader reflects on the multiplicity, variety, and subtlety of the factors which combine in varying ways and weights to induce persistency in social maladjustment, he will concede that the task of prevention has many ramifications; that it implicates fields of science in which knowledge is as yet far from complete; and that it touches upon almost all social institutions. It is, in a word, a highly complicated affair.

This is not a counsel of despair or pessimism; it is merely a call for the application of common sense and nondeceptive judgment to the results of our quest for solid facts and promising measures of prevention.

One point about which we must be realistic in planning a

program of delinquency prevention is that there are limits to effective action laid down by the general sociocultural situation. Children have to live in the world as it is; fundamental changes cannot be effectuated in a short space of time—too many special interests, prejudices, and values are involved. Nor can children be made good by removing evil out of their experience. Character is not built that way. For example, one does not get at the basic problems presented by the energetic, adventure-thirsty, mesomorphic lad by taking movies or comics away from him. If he has a need for such outlets he will somehow get to them; and deprivation is no cure. Direct police action against obvious evils, such as the peddling of drugs to children, is of course necessary. But, to the extent that general cultural pressures and disharmonies of our civilization may be involved in the background of anti-social behavior, we are confronted with a tremendous problem that can be managed only by society in general and an over-all social policy. This is difficult to achieve and would take years to evolve.

As one illustration of the immensity and difficulty of the general problem, we repeat what we said in 1930 in our first published work in this field, *Five Hundred Criminal Careers*:

After studying the careers of these five hundred young men and their families one is impelled to the ... conclusion that a critical evaluation of contemporary American ideals is necessary as a basis for the more intelligent moral guidance of our future citizens. That the uninteresting reiteration of moral precepts appears to be a failure in building character is becoming more and more clear. If we would build character in our youth and moor it to socially valuable ideals, something much more vital is needed. The youth of today can only be convinced and influenced by something that not only goes deeper, but is more appealing, than the ordinary church or Sunday-school routine. What that something is we do not know. Here is a field of research wherein social philosophers, the clergy, educators, social workers, and psychiatrists can join in fruitful and much needed study.[3]

When the above was written, most of the delinquents and young criminals of today were infants. It cannot be said that there has been much progress in improving that aspect of the general culture with which the above passage is concerned. And this is but one example of the slowness of cultural change in fundamentals.

But this fact need not make us pessimistic. For in the ultimate analysis, prevention of delinquent careers, as our findings suggest, is also dependent upon something more specific than the manipulation of the general cultural environment. It entails the structuring of *integrated personality and wholesome character during the first few formative years of life; and this, fortunately, is accomplished largely in the home.* Although basic modifications in the general system of habits and values that permeate our culture are bound to be slow, we can take advantage of the oft-neglected fact that parents are to a great extent not only the bearers, but also the *selective filters,* of the general culture. The same is true of school-teachers, with whom children spend much of their time during the most impressionable and formative stages of life. Thus, there is both realism and promise in taking more direct and specific steps to improve the *under-the-roof culture* in home and school.[4]

Types of Preventive Programs

Programs of delinquency prevention are classifiable into (1) those dealing with very general socioeconomic conditions that affect an entire culture and are therefore but remotely

[3] New York, Alfred A. Knopf, 1930, pp. 337-338.

[4] We do not of course deny the value of community efforts at crime control; these can be improved by a better definition of specific goals derived from differentiative traits of delinquents and nondelinquents.

related to delinquency; (2) those which, though not organized chiefly to cope with delinquency, still have a natural, albeit indirect and incidental, relationship to the problem; and (3) those which are set up to deal specifically with the conditions that presumably make for delinquency.

European criminologists have generally recommended the first type of attack, couching their suggestions for crime-preventive measures in general terms. But while there can be little quarrel, for example, with such a generalization as that "Every measure that helps to make the people physically, mentally, and economically healthier is a weapon in the struggle against the world of crime,"[5] it is too remote from the factors specifically involved in the social evil of delinquency and crime to be of much practical value.

As for the second type of crime-preventive activity, although it is much closer to the operative details of the problem, it is still not specially designed to cope with it. It has been pointed out by Lukas, who has given much study to the problem, that "Except for the police, children's courts, and reformatory institutions, public and private agencies are not organized primarily for the prevention of crime and delinquency. That function is considered to be an adjunct to or a by-product of their other related purposes. Direct services, designed mainly as crime preventives, are few; the indirect services are many."[6] He adds that since such "fairly typical indirect preventive services" as wholesome recreation, good housing, good schools, and the like "can contribute a vital and significant force in the lives of everyone," they have "justifiably had claimed for them the function of contributing to delinquency . . . prevention."[7] While this is true, the data of the

[5] Aschaffenburg, G., *Crime and Its Repression* (Boston: Modern Criminal Science Series, No. 6, 1913), p. 228.

[6] Lukas, E. J., "Prevention of Crime," in Branham, V. C., and Kutash, S. B., *Encyclopedia of Criminology* (New York: Philosophical Library), p. 333. This thoughtful article can be of help to all who contemplate preventive programs.

[7] *Ibid.*

present study indicate how much more pointed the approach to the problem of prevention must be. That socioeconomic measures for general improvement of the lot of the underprivileged are desirable cannot be gainsaid; but their exact contribution to the prevention of delinquency is hard to assess: the same underprivileged status in which the families of our delinquents found themselves was also the lot of the nondelinquents' families.

The third type of delinquency preventive program is designed, specifically, to cope with the problems of discovering and dealing with the forces and situations, inside and outside the child, that are commonly found associated with predelinquency and delinquency.

The specific clues to prevention disclosed in the preceding chapters suggest clearly defined targets at which to aim specific programs to supplement that shotgun attack on general socioeconomic evils which is made with a hope and a prayer that, as regards the prevention of delinquency, a few of the pellets will somehow hit the right spots.

Specific Targets of Delinquency Prevention

In reflecting upon the major findings of the foregoing chapters, it is evident that the primary focus of interest must be on (a) the traits and characteristics of the delinquent himself, (b) the family life, (c) the school, and (d) the employment of leisure time.

(a) THE DELINQUENT HIMSELF. What can be done, specifically, about the constitution, traits, and characteristics that distinguish delinquents as a group from nondelinquents?

The greater incidence of mesomorphic constitutional physique among delinquents, and the "growth spurt" of these boys at thirteen to fourteen years, provide targets for specific action. The excess of mesomorphy among delinquents as a class ought to suggest to all persons and agencies intimately concerned with the guidance of youth—parents, teachers, community recreational agencies, and others—that special allowance must be made in all major channels of self-expression for the greater energy output of certain boys, if their drives are not to take antisocial expression. The days of "winning the West," of the whaling ship, and of other fields of action for energetic, adventure-hungry youth are no more. To supply legitimate substitutes is a challenge to the ingenuity of schools, recreational authorities, and vocational guides. There is obviously a need for greater variety in curriculum patterns, in leisure-time programs and in vocational opportunities, and a more specific fitting of types of boys into areas of activity.

The greater inclination of the delinquents to the practical, concrete forms of mental activity and their disinclination to abstract, verbalistic intellectual processes furnish specific targets for designers of school curricula. In regard to such qualitative intellectual traits as incapacity for objective interests, unrealistic thinking, lack of "common sense," and unsystematic approach to mental problems, those who plan curricula need to consult with experts in clinical psychiatry and psychology, because such traits are especially entangled with emotional tendencies.

In weighing the characteristics of delinquents as derived from the Rorschach Test and psychiatric interview, school and clinic have the greatest opportunity for action directed toward specific goals. These are so clearly of a nature to interfere with a satisfactory taming of primitive impulses and to facilitate uncontrolled, unthinking antisocial self-expression, that they furnish specific targets for preventive activities on the part of family clinics and school agencies. Among them, it will be recalled, are assertiveness, defiance of or ambivalence to authority; excessive feelings of hostility, suspiciousness, destructiveness; unconventionality in ideas and behavior oral-receptive and sadistic-destructive trends; marked emotional impulsiveness, and defective self-control; sensuality and acquisitiveness; deficiency in conscientiousness and self-criticism; preponderance of extroversive trends and/or the tendency to resolve emotional conflicts by an impulsive "acting out."

Such traits tell their own story as to why it is that so frequently the efforts of juvenile courts and other agencies dealing with delinquents, devoted and intelligent as these often are, can accomplish so little in changing a course of habitual antisocial conduct. The deep-seated nature of the temperamental and character traits found to differentiate persistent delinquents from nondelinquents, and the extremely early age at which delinquents first manifest marked difficulties in adjustment as expressed in misbehavior, should make us realize how absolutely essential it is for schools, particularly, to be equipped to discover *potential* delinquents before the trends of maladaptive behavior become too fixed. For the schools are in a strategic position to note such marked deviations and difficulties of adaptation at the age of around six when the child first enters grade school. *Character prophylaxis*—the testing of children early and periodically to detect malformations of emotional development at a stage when the twig can still be bent—is as necessary as are early and periodic medical examinations. A crying need of the times in this field is a *preventive medicine of personality and character*.

(*b*) FAMILY LIFE. Many crucial differences were found between the parents of the delinquents and those of the other boys—the greater intellectual and emotional abnormalities of the delinquents' grandparents (and other distant relatives) and parents, the higher incidence of alcoholism and criminalism in the families in which the parents of the delinquent boys had themselves been reared; their more extensive physical, intellectual, and emotional handicaps, as well as drunkenness and criminalism; their greater dependence on various social welfare agencies. All this suggests that the community must somehow break the vicious circle of charac-ter-damaging influences on children exerted by parents who are themselves the distorted personality products of adverse parental influences. This can be done only through inten-sive instruction of each generation of prospective parents in the elements of mental hygiene and the requisites of happy and healthy family life. It calls for a tremendous multiplica-tion of psychiatric, social, religious, educational, and other community resources for improving the basic equipment of present and prospective parents in the assumption of a whole-some parental role. For there cannot be the slightest doubt, in the light of the facts marshaled in the preceding pages, that it is futile to treat the child, delinquent or otherwise, apart from the family that contributes much to make him what he is. Without concentration on the family, particularly the parents, we may set up boys' clubs, recreational centers, clinics, and the like, and we may inveigh against the movies, comics, and crime-suggesting toys; but we shall still be trying to sweep back the tide of childhood maladjustment and de-linquency with pitifully inadequate brooms.

Parents are not born with a knowledge of how to bring up children; if they were, there would be far less delinquency. Under modern conditions of city life, especially in the under-privileged areas, what used to be a problem that tended to take care of itself in rural and semirural America, when families were large, cultural ideas and ideals more uniform, and life simpler, has become difficult and perplexing. It is obvious that little progress can be made in the prevention of juvenile delinquency until family life is strengthened through a large-scale, pervasive, continuous program designed to bring to bear all the resources of mental hygiene, social work, educa-tion, and religious and ethical teaching upon this central issue.

The differentiative traits of the parents of our boys lead to the conclusion that all the community's agencies for the guidance of young people in the proper selection of mates and in preparation for marriage—agencies specializing in marital problems, church groups, family welfare organizations—need to enlarge and enrich their techniques.

The evidences of disruption in the family life of delinquents are specific targets at which to aim. To cite but one illustration—if agencies interested in the recreational movement, boys' clubs, and other methods for constructive use of leisure were to formulate their plans and activities around a working principle of encouraging recreations that would engage the interest of the family as a unit, this one principle alone might serve to counteract the tendency to family disintegration. Beginning with the cementing influence of family-group recreation, the path might be opened to improvement in other constituents of the unhealthy family pattern.

It will be recalled that certain other unwholesome parent-child relationships, apart from those already noted, were found strikingly to differentiate the family atmosphere of delinquents and nondelinquents. Far more of their homes were broken; far more of the mothers of the delinquents allowed their children to shift for themselves during leisure hours; far fewer of their fathers evinced sympathy and affection for their boys; and while there was much more warmth on the part of the mothers generally, fewer of the delinquents' mothers had a healthily affectionate relationship to the boys. Far fewer of the delinquents were, in turn, warmly attached to their fathers and mothers; a far lower percentage of the delinquent boys accepted their fathers as desirable models for emulation; to a greater extent the former believed that neither of the parents was genuinely concerned for their welfare; and the disciplinary practices of the parents of the delinquents were far less adequate.

Here is a dynamic area of intrafamily crosscurrents that in large measure accounts for the persistent maladjustment of the boys who became delinquent. Again we have a situation which, though highly involved and complex, might be attacked by concentrating on a series of specific constituents of the entire emotion-laden area. If, for example, there were community agencies to instruct parents systematically in regard to the emotional significance of various disciplinary practices and to demonstrate to them how behavior situations usually improve when discipline is fair and firm and unaccompanied by anger, they might learn to adopt such practices with socializing effect on their children. Again, if parents were systematically taught simple elements of the dynamics of parent-child relationships; of the struggle the young child must go through in adjusting his instinctual drives and their emotional accompaniments in relation to mother, father, and brothers and sisters; of the role of the father as the first "ego-ideal," and, in general, of the great part played by early parent-child experiences in the crystallization of the child's basic personality and character traits which will be carried into adulthood and become more difficult to modify with the passage of time, some headway might be made in rendering intrafamily life more hygienic and happy.

The problem is enormous in scope. It calls for the widespread cooperative endeavor of child-guidance clinics, schoolteachers, family welfare agencies, church and other communal resources. In most communities it will be found that there are not enough facilities, such as clinics, and that the effort of public and private agencies is not planfully articulated so as to give the most economical results.

(c) THE SCHOOL. A great deal of time, and at a very impressionable age, is spent by children in schools. Our findings have shown that much more goes on in the intraschool situation than the mere commerce in ideas about "readin', writin', and 'rithmetic," and that what does transpire is of an essentially emotional nature. On the part of the teacher, she cannot altogether get rid of her own emotional problems through the channel of drilling students in the curriculum. On the part of the little pupils, they do not, when they enter the classroom, leave behind their emotional freight, their worries about parental anger, neglect, drunkenness, criminalism.

We have seen that delinquent boys largely possess certain temperamental and personality traits and special abilities and disabilities which distinguish them from the general run of nondelinquents. We have also seen that because of the poor parent-child relationships predominating in delinquents' families the boys have difficulty in finding an emotionally sympathetic adult as a symbol for emulation around whom ideals and standards of behavior can be woven to form the core of character. Such facts—and there are other relevant ones— suggest that fundamental changes in school curricula and teacher training must be made.

Forcing certain types of children into the traditional mold results in increasing tension, frustration, revolt, and delinquency. Much greater flexibility in school curricula is called for; a rich variety of satisfying school experiences must be devised which will enlist the interests of different types of children.

To supply teachers with the necessary "know-how" for coping with the emotional problems of childhood, teacher training will have to be modified to include liberal elements of dynamic psychology and opportunities to participate in clinical conferences. Practice teaching of the various subjects in the curriculum cannot replace the need for an understanding of the troubles and tensions of children as they wrestle with the problem of adjusting to the taming restraints of the adult world.

More important, school authorities will have to recognize the role of teachers as parent-substitutes and ego-ideals in the case of many children. Perhaps young-adult male teachers are needed in greater number, even in the kindergarten and elementary grades. Perhaps husband-wife teams of teachers would provide a more natural and wholesome emotional climate in the classroom. At all events, experiments are needed to test out various patterns of teacher-child relationships from the point of view of their effect on the dynamics of temperament and emotion and the formation of integrated personality and acceptable character.

The existing great shortage of teachers presents a serious social problem in itself; to attract the kind of teachers who will be skilled in coping with the emotional difficulties of childhood, a far higher social evaluation of the role of the teacher will have to be brought about.

The marked differences between the delinquent boys and their nondelinquent counterparts again afford specific targets at which to direct preventive action in this area: Among the delinquents as a group there was more school retardation, poorer scholastic achievement, greater dislike of school, less academic ambition, greater preference for adventurous activities. But these traits are not essentially chargeable to a difference in general intelligence, for the two groups were similar in average I.Q. Their true roots are apparent from the other differentiative traits and behavior manifestations in which the delinquents were different from the other lads: They did not adjust themselves as well to their schoolmates; almost all the delinquents, compared to but 86 of the other lads, indulged in all forms of misconduct in school, ranging from defiance, stubbornness, lying, and persistent inattention to truancy, stealing, and sexual misconduct. It will be recalled, further, that while such misbehavior occurred at eight or less among a third of the delinquents (their average age at first school misbehavior having been 9.5 years), it occurred as early as this among less than a tenth of the few nondelinquents who had misbehaved in school (their average age at first misconduct in school having been 12.5 years).

These facts suggest not only that a boy's school misconduct

as a harbinger (and sometimes an accompanier) of misconduct in the general community is not only of emotional origin,
but that the emotional difficulties are deep-rooted, reaching
into the most tender years. When, to the early age of first
school misconduct is added the early age of first anti-legal
behavior (almost half the delinquents were only eight at the
time), it becomes clearer than ever that the evidences of persistent delinquency arise essentially before puberty and that
the elementary school therefore stands in the front line of
attack on the problem.

In an enlightened educational system the school could
function as the litmus paper of personality and character
maladaption, reflecting early in the child's growth the acid
test of his success or failure in his first attempts to cope with
the problems of life posed by a restrictive society and code of
behavior. In such a system, the best psychiatric, psychologic,
medical, social, and other facilities would then be focused on
the specific traits shown to be most largely related to personality distortion and maladapted behavior at a critical point
in the child's development when character and habit are still
sufficiently plastic for effective therapeutic intervention.

The intricacies of the problem of early recognition and
treatment of delinquency, and a chief reason why so little has
been accomplished toward its solution, is shown by the simple
fact that when a child first begins to display signs of maladaptation it is very difficult to say whether these are true danger
signals of persistent delinquency to come or are merely
transient phenomena of the youngster's trying of his wings.
Bits of maladapted and even antisocial behavior at this early
stage are not necessarily symptomatic of future delinquency.
It therefore becomes of prime importance to devise a method
of distinguishing, very early in life, those children who are
headed for delinquent careers in order that therapeutic
measures may be timely and effective.

Is there a sufficiently reliable instrumentality for making

this crucially important distinction between the potentially delinquent child and the child who will probably soon outgrow his difficulties of adaptation?

Our study of many hundreds of factors distinguishing actual persistent delinquents from nondelinquents has made possible the construction of such an instrument which gives every promise of being effective. It has been possible to develop a series of *prognostic tables* derived (1) from the data of the family background of the two sets of boys, (2) from the revelations of the Rorschach Test, and (3) from the psychiatric interviews with the boys. With the use of such devices it ought to be possible to determine, at the point of school entrance, even before the display of most of the overt symptoms of what appears to be a tendency to persistent antisocial behavior, which children are probably headed in the direction of delinquency. (For details, see *Unraveling Juvenile Delinquency,* Chapter XX.)

The principle of such prognostic instruments is simple. Just as insurance companies determine the amount of premium to charge in different classes of life insurance by correlating such factors as age, health, occupation, and the like with actual longevity of different classes of persons in thousands of cases, so it is feasible to predict with reasonable accuracy the chances that a child presenting certain traits and characteristics will be a delinquent or a nondelinquent.

A review of the factors of difference emerging from the family and personal history of the delinquents and nondelinquents makes it clear that those which were operative prior to school entrance were largely in the area of interpersonal relations within the family group. Since we are interested primarily in prognostic devices which would help to identify potential delinquents upon or soon after school entrance, selection of the factors had first to be narrowed to those operable prior to school entrance. For this reason, we excluded, for example, the factor of gang membership, because few boys as young as six are already members of gangs, and the factor of broken homes, which, though sharply differentiating the delinquent from the nondelinquent somewhat later, was as yet an incompleted factor when the boys entered school.

From among all possibly applicable factors, those in which the greatest difference was found to exist between the delinquents and the nondelinquents had then to be determined. Next, we had to consider whether or not these factors were mutually exclusive and, if possible, to select those which were more likely to be independent of one another. (We have, however, learned from experience that even if there is some overlapping of factors the value of the resulting instrumentality for predictive purposes is not fundamentally impaired.) This selective process permitted us to use five factors in the construction of a prognostic instrument based upon social data: discipline of boy by father, supervision of boy by mother, affection of father for boy, affection of mother for boy, cohesiveness of family.

If the reader will review some of the other distinguishing but less differentiative factors in the family background, he will see that it is possible to construct other prognostic tables, even though it would probably require the cumulative weight of more than five such factors to yield as high a predictive power as those afforded by the five we have used. This is an illustration of a fundamental idea discussed in the preceding chapter: the concept of multiple causation. In other words, it is not merely one syndrome of the five most highly differentiative social (or any other) factors that yields the greatest prognostic possibility because of high causal weight, but also other syndromes or patterns. We have here a sort of interchangeable "coin of the realm" of causation, in which a certain number of external and/or internal pressures of one kind may just as readily incline a boy to delinquency as a larger (or smaller) number of pressures of another kind. It is the task of the therapist in the individual case to uncover and remove or modify as many of these pressures as possible in order to permit the particular child to function on a relatively even keel without, on the one hand, becoming too neurotic or, on the other, becoming a persistent delinquent.

Prognostic tables similar to the one above described were also prepared on the basis of five of the most differentiative character traits brought out by the Rorschach Test and five temperamental traits revealed through the psychiatric examinations. Use of all three types of tables would enhance prognostic power; but these latter of course require technically trained psychologists and psychiatrists to administer the examinations and apply the predictions, while teachers and social workers can more readily apply the table based on family background factors.

Prognostic tables should of course not be used mechanically, automatically, or as a substitute for sound clinical judgment. They are merely intended to help in considering the problems of an individual child in the perspective of organized experience with hundreds of other boys who in many respects resemble or differ from the lad under consideration. As to some factors, each child of course remains unique; but such qualities, and their significance in the total situation, are exceedingly difficult to determine and assess. The dimensions and depths of each child's problems can be much more accurately appraised by seeing them in the light of the background picture of hundreds of other children, than they can be if the investigator or therapist relies exclusively on "good guesses" or "clinical hunch."

The prognostic tables should not be used even by clinical experts until they have been tested on other samples of children than those embraced in this research. As a distinguished authority on biometrics, statistics, and public health has put it, "A priori argument [as to the value or validity of such prognostic instrumentalities] will not get far, howsoever it be extended. What one needs is trial and observation."[8]

(d) LEISURE TIME. In their life on the city streets, as well as in the other respects noted, we have seen that the delinquent boys are worse off than the nondelinquents: Their families moved about more frequently, interfering with whatever stabilizing influences there are in attachment and loyalty to a definite community. To a greater extent than the nondelinquent lads, the delinquents worked in street trades where they were subject to the hazards of unsupervised employment at an impressionable age. Their recreational as well as work preferences were for risky and adventurous energy outlets, reflected not only in excessive truck hopping, keeping late hours, bunking out, running away from home, destroying property, and the like, but also in seeking out play places at a considerable distance from their homes, and other enticing locales of risk and adventure such as railroad yards and waterfronts. These tendencies are also shown in the greater extent to which the delinquents had serious street accidents and even (vicariously) in their much more frequent movie attendance. Most of the delinquents became gang members, and many preferred companions older than themselves. There is also strong evidence that the delinquents disliked the confinement of playgrounds, supervised recreations, or attendance at clubs or other centers which they rarely joined of their own desire. Finally, they were more neglectful of church attendance than the nondelinquents.

Here we have a series of behavior manifestations that unquestionably suggest that settlement houses, school community centers, church centers, boys' clubs, and other agencies must take into account the preferences of these adventure-thirsty boys who dislike intensive supervision and tend to turn to delinquency as a congenial way of life. Such agencies

[8] Edwin Bidwell Wilson, "Prediction," book review in "A Symposium on *Unraveling Juvenile Delinquency,*" Harvard Law Review, 1951, pp. 1022, 1041.

should experiment with various means of attracting and guiding youngsters of this type into at least socially harmless, if not positively constructive, channels. In a busy, exciting, urban community of individualists "on the make," these boys drift among the general population unattached by loyalties except to those of similar energy drive and consuming interest. There is obviously a crying social need for coping with this problem through well-planned community action, based upon careful surveys of local conditions, liabilities, facilities, and needs. A number of communities have made promising beginnings in this direction.[9]

Throughout the foregoing analysis our purpose has been to emphasize fundamental ideas—the better aiming of preventive efforts at more specific targets. We have not attempted to go into detail about techniques to be used in boys' clubs, other social agencies, juvenile courts, probation, and the like.

Nor have we found it feasible to pigeonhole the relevant targets for action into those which the school should *exclusively* be charged with, those which are the sole responsibility of the church, those which are the private domain of the clinic, those which some other community agencies should alone deal with. Reflection upon the nature of the problem shows that, while each of the agencies has a job to do, the specific traits and characteristics to be coped with do not neatly fall into institutional compartments. All that can be said is that the school or the clinic or some other agency should be charged with a leading, if not the primary, responsibility in this or that area; but just as the separate identity of each factor or target does not destroy the organic unity

9 See Glueck and Glueck (Editors) *Preventing Crime* (New York: McGraw-Hill Book Co., Inc., 1936); "Report of the Committee on Crime Prevention of the American Prison Association" (New York: American Prison Association, October, 1942); Tappan, P. W., *Juvenile Delinquency* (New York: McGraw-Hill Book Co., Inc., 1949), pp. 490 *et seq.*; Carr, L. J., *Delinquency Control* (New York: Harper & Brothers, 1950), Part IV.

of the person-situation,[10] so the specialization of each agency in one group of factors does not eliminate the harmonious participation of all community agencies in a well-conceived general plan of attack.[11]

We have not attempted in this book to make detailed suggestions as to how a community should go about the task of organizing clinics, establishing and improving premarital and marital guidance centers, and the like. There are some useful publications which the interested citizen can consult for such practical matters. To name but a few, we may refer to *Preventing Crime,*[12] a symposium of some of the more promising programs in different parts of the United States organized under the headings of "Coordinated Community Programs," "School Programs," "Police Programs," "Intra-Mural Guidance Programs," "Extra-Mural Guidance Programs," "Boys' Clubs," and "Recreational Programs;" the "Report of the Committee on Crime Prevention of the American Prison Association, 1942";[13] Carr's well-documented guidebook on *Delinquency Control,*[14] with the very useful part on "Social Action," which gives a blueprint and clearly defined ideas regarding organization, procedure, and division of labor;[15] the reports of the National Conference on Prevention and Control of Juvenile Delinquency held in Washington in the fall of 1946;[16] the publications of the White House Con-

[10] A leading pioneer in the study of crime long ago pointed to a basic truism: "The criminal act in every instance is the resultant interaction between a particularly constituted personality and a particular environment." —Glueck, Bernard, *First Annual Report of the Psychiatric Clinic, Sing Sing Prison,* Mental Hygiene, Vol. 2, 1918, p. 12.

[11] See Lukas, *op. cit.,* p. 334, on the value of coordination of the efforts of all community agencies.

[12] Edited by Sheldon and Eleanor Glueck. New York: McGraw-Hill Book Co., Inc., 1936.

[13] American Prison Association, 135 East Fifteenth St., New York. There are other valuable publications of the Association.

[14] Revised Edition. New York: Harper & Brothers, 1950.

[15] Compare, also, Carr's method of predicting juvenile delinquency with ours. *Op. cit.,* pp. 163 *et seq.*

[16] Publications are available from the Superintendent of Documents, Government Printing Office, Washington, D.C.

ference on child welfare, the various Yearbooks of the National Probation and Parole Association;[17] and the more recent, thoughtful textbooks on criminology, such as Taft's *Criminology, A Cultural Interpretation*[18] and Tappan's *Juvenile Delinquency*.[19] This list by no means exhausts the sources of sound practical advice related to findings of fact; it is merely a guide to the reader who is interested in the strategy and tactics of community effort for delinquency control.

But let us once more caution that delinquency cannot be coped with through prejudices about this or that "ology" or "cause," or through purblind faith in some simple nostrum. Nor is it likely that some inspired researcher will soon come up with a brilliant yet simple idea in the manner of Archimedes' sudden inspiration in the bathtub. Yet we trust that those who see this problem in the true perspective of its immense perplexity and its tangled ramifications will not despair. There is soundly based hope in the fact that persistent delinquency is usually not inevitable. There has been much futile argument throughout the ages about the puzzle of freedom of will versus determinism. The argument has largely misfired because it has dealt with the question in the abstract: Does Man have freedom of will, or is he the slave of deterministic forces? The practical issue is the extent to which the particular *individual* under consideration has capacity for purposive self-direction. Individuals differ in this, largely on the basis of the limits laid down genetically and their potentialities under favorable environmental circumstances. It is the function of parents, teachers, clinicians, and others who have to do with children to remove as many of the stifling "deterministic" ashes as possible so that the spark of "freedom" in

17 Such as *Dealing with Delinquency*, 1940 (Edited by Marjorie Bell). New York: The National Probation and Parole Association, 1790 Broadway.
18 Revised Edition. New York: The Macmillan Co., 1950.
19 New York: McGraw Hill Book Co., 1949.

the above sense may be achieved by the particular individual to the fullest extent of his genetically anchored potentialities. Except in the most extreme cases, it should be possible to modify character and the environmental pressures that distort character, if early, relevant, and sufficiently patient measures are taken.

In the meantime, we have one source of comfort that should stimulate research and experimentation. Determinism does not mean fatalism; it refers to the observed fact that nature presents a routine series of events linked together in what we call causal sequence. This does not mean that we are unable to intervene to change a familiar sequence by therapeutic and prophylactic methods that "hit the bull's eye." In other words, *in delinquency we are dealing not with predestination but with destination.* And experiments have demonstrated that there is a probability that in many cases destination can be redirected by pointed and specific early intervention.

If we recognize that this problem is not merely one of "bad" boys needing to be punished to make them "good," or even of misled boys needing to be treated kindly to make them "reform,"[20] but rather of disorders of temperament, personality, and character with an even more complex causative system than exists in many diseases, we will at least approach the problem with an *attitude* and an *insight* that give every promise of the ultimate achievement of effective remedies and preventive programs.

Such an attitude and such an insight may be summed up simply in the recognition that in the eyes of science there are no "good boys" or "bad boys," but only children who need less help in growing up and those who need more.

[20] On this type of approach see the thoughtful analysis of results of an experiment in preventive therapy, in Powers, E., and Witmer, H., *An Experiment in the Prevention of Delinquency* (New York: Columbia University Press, 1951).

Index

212 DELINQUENTS IN THE MAKING

Child guidance, 1, 14, 179-180
Childhood misbehavior, 6-7
Church attendance, 92
Circular reasoning, 16
"Clinical hunch," 207
Cohesiveness, family, 53-54
Companions, 2, 88-90, 178, 207
Comparison of delinquents and non-delinquents, 37
Complacent factors, 172
Compulsory trends, 158
Conant, J., 165
Conditioning, childhood, 4, 103, 179-180
Conduct standards of home, 49-50
Conflicts, emotional, 134-137
    methods of resolving, 136-137
Constitution and delinquency, 2, 14-15, 100-102
Contagion, immunity to, 108
Control group, 13
Controlled social situation, 177
Conventionality, 155
Convictions of delinquents, 12
Cooperativeness, 150
Court appearances of delinquents, 12
Crime causation, see Causation of delinquency (crime)
Criminalism in families, 40, 41-42, 49
Crowding in homes, 58
Culture, and delinquency, 3-4, 93, 179-180, 186, 208
    conflict, 2, 57
Cultural refinement, 48
Cunningham, M., 38n

Deep-rootedness of antisocial habits, 80
Defensive-attitude, 152
Defiance, 144, 167
Definitions, 18
Delinquency, areas, 28, 87, 189
    deep-seated nature of, 197, 203
    early recognition of, 203-204
    knot of, 184
    potential, 197
    prediction of, 204-207
    rates, 38-39
    riddle of, 164-188
Delinquent child, definition of, 6, 10-11
Determinism, 211
"Deviates," 10
"Differential association" as supposed basic cause of delinquency, 89
Disciplinary practices, 65-66, 200
Disharmony, body, 99-100
Disproportions, body, 98-100

Drunkenness, 40, 41, 49
Ears, condition of boys', 111
Ecologic study of delinquency, 3
Economic condition of boys' homes, 40, 43-45, 49
    studies of crime, 4
Ectomorphy, 15, 101, 186
Education of boys, 70-74
    grandparents, 40
    parents, 43
"Ego-ideal," 89, 178, 183, 200, 201, 202
Emotional attitudes, 174
    conflicts, 134-137
    disturbances of members of parental families, 40, 41
    parents, 43
    boys, 76-77, 80, 134-137, 145-149
    lability, 157-158
    control, 158
Employment of boys, 83-84
    fathers, 44
    mothers, 51
Endocrine glands, 173
Endomorphy, 15, 101
Energy of delinquents, 97, 102, 137, 175, 178
Enuresis, 107, 116, 173
Environment and heredity, 75, 172
    individual, 93
Ethnic derivation, 12, 39
Excitement, search of, by boys, 85-88
Expectations, meeting of others', 155
Extroversion-introversion, 159, 175
Eyes, condition of boys', 111

Failure, fear of, 148
Family, atmosphere, 68, 197-198
    background, 13-14
    conduct standards of, 41, 43, 46, 49-50, 182
    disorganization, 53, 59-61, 183
    economic status of, 46, 182
    emotional climate of, 53, 58, 182
    pride, 48-49
    recreation, 52-53, 199
    responsibilities, 42-45
    size of boys', 57-58
    parents', 40
Fathers, affection of, for boys, 61-63, 199
    work habits of, 46
Five Hundred Criminal Careers, 192-193
Forced marriages, 43, 56
Foreign birth of parents, 57
Freedom of will, 211
Freud, S., 62, 63
Frustration, feeling of, 148-149

1942
1